*For Josephine and Jules*

# Contents

Contents

# List of Figures and Tables

## Figures

## Tables

# Acknowledgments

We would like to acknowledge the support and contribution of a number of people to our work and thinking in developing this text. First, we thank Paul Goodwin for checking the sense of our simplified quantitative option appraisal format in Chapter 6, and acknowledge his contribution through earlier joint publications. Ron Bradfield provided us with sources of information as we wrote, and has contributed to our thinking on scenario method over a number of years. Martyna Śliwa worked with us in developing the concept of the critical scenario method (CSM) that we set out in Chapter 5. We must acknowledge the contribution of Kees van der Heijden to our early understanding of scenario method during the time that we worked with him at Strathclyde University, UK.

In developing our thinking, we have drawn upon the earlier work of a number of scholars. In relation to scenario methods, we have been informed by the writings of Pierre Wack and Paul Schoemaker in particular. In developing our thinking on the integration of stakeholder analysis, we have drawn upon the thinking of Ed Freeman. Our integration of stakeholder analysis into a framework for considering issues of power, business ethics and social responsibility has been further informed and inspired by the writing of Bent Flyvbjerg.

Whilst all these people have contributed to our thinking in developing this text, we must take personal responsibility for the final print – in particular, any omissions or errors that we have allowed to creep in.

*Durham*                                                    GEORGE WRIGHT

*Melbourne*                                               GEORGE CAIRNS

# Introduction

## HOW THIS BOOK IS ORGANIZED

At its core, this book presents a detailed step-by-step account of the "intuitive logics" method of scenario thinking. Linked to this core, we detail a range of methodological innovations and show how to apply the most relevant technique to a particular situation. Our approach is based on a mix of both high-level research and top-level consultancy experience. The focus of our book is on the demonstration and illustration of practical steps in scenario development processes.

The book describes the logical bases of a range of scenario methods and provides detailed "road maps" on how to implement them, together with practical examples of their application. We review the strengths and weaknesses of each method, and detail the time and material resources that each method requires.

## KEY INNOVATIONS

This book offers various key innovations to existing books on scenario method. It provides a detailed, step-by-step, approach to enable the reader to create scenarios without the aid of an experienced scenario practitioner. It enables development of a broader range of scenarios that include more extreme futures than those that are produced using conventional scenario practice. As such, organizations can become prepared for a broader range of futures, including those of low predictability.

Our book incorporates focused consideration of the full range of stakeholders who will be affected by the occurrence of events within particular scenario storylines – ranging from those stakeholders with direct self-interest, motivation and power to influence events within a particular scenario, to those who are marginal or powerless and often excluded from consideration. In this way, our approach can be used for the explicit analysis of issues of corporate social responsibility.

We evaluate alternative organizational strategies, including those that are flexible and diversified, and those that are less adaptable and are, thus, more exposed in the face of discontinuous change

The book combines qualitative approaches with basic numeric decision analysis approaches. It presents ways of assessing "organizational receptiveness" to the development of future scenarios that may portray bleak, inhospitable futures and/or directly challenge business-as-usual thinking; and presents real-world case illustrations of the methods and approaches that are contained in the book.

These innovations will enable you to be more aware of, and prepared for, alternative futures. Our book is designed to be of interest to practicing managers across a broad spectrum of organizations and to policy-makers in the political and public sector arenas with regard to assisting strategic analysis. We explain and justify the academic basis of our practice-based recommendations.

## OVERVIEW OF CONTENT AND APPROACH

### Chapter 1: Why Should the Individual and the Organization Practice Scenario Thinking?

We document the prevalence of business-as-usual thinking in organizations: the common-place notion that the future will be a simple extrapolation of the past. We outline the "intuitive logics" method of scenario thinking and argue that it provides the individual and the organization with a means to challenge conventional thought. After introducing the basic principles of scenario thinking, we discuss the criticism that scenario method is basically an "art" that lacks theoretical underpinning and methodological rigor. We show that this viewpoint gives pre-eminence to science-based methods over intuitive thought. We argue that this perspective, which underpins the "rational school" of strategic analysis, fails to engage with existence of the "social construction of reality" and the centrality of power in decision-making. As such, the science-based perspective on strategic analysis is, in itself, fragile and bounded in its rationality. Scenario thinking provides structure to intuitive thought and also provides challenge to initial intuitions, such that higher-level intuition is developed.

## Chapter 2: Working with Scenarios: Introducing the Basic Method

In this chapter, we set out the various stages and options for undertaking scenario development. We offer approaches to creating scenarios that range from individual options for analysis in response to a complex problem within a constrained time frame, to the use of the "scenario method" by groups of diverse organizational members and stakeholders working together over a period of weeks or months. Whichever approach is adopted, we provide a set of basic ground rules that set the context for challenge to business-as-usual thinking that avoids inter-personal challenge and conflict between managers. Overall, we set out the detailed stages of the intuitive logics scenario method.

## Chapter 3: Incorporating Stakeholder Values and Facilitating Critique of Scenario Storylines

We discuss deficiencies in conventional scenario practice – in its inability to offer challenge to the mental frames that typically solidify in scenario construction, shown by predictability in participants' choice of scenario elements, theme selections, and focus on current high-profile issues and concerns. We show that constructed scenarios are often limited by either replicating participants' current concerns as future concerns, or failing to consider the impact of future events upon all affected stakeholders. We then consider how to break the mold of scenario participants' thinking. We do this by introducing a mixture of techniques that challenge current framing of issues, and enable the step-by-step development of a broadened range of scenarios. Our methods include role-playing stakeholder perspectives as they react to unfolding scenario events, and the use of devil's advocacy and dialectical inquiry, to critique the content of scenario storylines that are in development.

## Chapter 4: Understanding Stakeholder Viewpoints

We develop the stakeholder approach to incorporate the "broad" stakeholder viewpoint – considering the impact of different possible futures on all affected stakeholders, including those who lack power or whose interests may not be immediately apparent where the scenario process is narrowly focused on the organization and its interests. We introduce an enhanced scenario approach that embeds consideration of the interests and impacts of the future upon the broadest range of stakeholders. We see such a critical scenario method as being of particular relevance and value in the socially-responsible, contemporary world – a world of high-profile corporate scandals, potentially devastating climate change, and the emergence of the ethical investor and consumer.

## Chapter 5: Augmented Scenario Approaches: Delving Deeper and Stretching Wider

We detail two ways of augmenting the basic intuitive logics scenario method to provide deeper insights into the future. In the first augmentation, we demonstrate how to elicit the extreme outcomes of the resolution of previously identified driving forces, and show how this material can be used as an additional resource for subsequent scenario storyline development. In the second augmentation, we provide the detailed steps of the critical scenario method and, using a case example, demonstrate how to analyze the impact of events upon those stakeholders with a direct involvement and interest who can affect the situation, and also upon the broader range of stakeholders, who may be affected by decisions and actions, both now and in the future.

## Chapter 6: Scenarios and Decision Analysis

Having set out a framework for assessing strategic options, we now discuss how it is often psychologically difficult for individual decision-makers to evaluate the robustness of strategy against constructed scenarios. The holistic thinking that is required to support effective decision-making may be hindered by mental obstacles – for example, "lexicographic ranking" – where undue attention is paid to particular strategic objectives at the expense of others. As a remedy, we propose the use of "hard" multi-attribute decision analysis as a complement to "soft" scenario method. This combination of approaches allows a more formal method of strategy evaluation against a range of constructed scenarios.

## Chapter 7: Creating Robust Strategies and Robust Organizations

We demonstrate how to combine scenario thinking with options thinking, to allow the organization to make effective decisions and plans in the face of low levels of predictability. We demonstrate that the decision-maker should be alert to the degree to which a strategic option provides strategic defense and strategic opportunism in the face of high-impact events of low predictability. Here, we take the scenario process beyond simply considering what might feasibly happen in the broad environment to address the key question that is frequently posed by decision-makers In the face of multiple futures: "So what?" Our prescription presents an action framework that can be implemented by decision-makers as a check-list in undertaking option evaluation against the range of constructed scenarios. As such, it provides the "missing link" between what the future may hold and what the organization should do.

## Chapter 8: The Backwards Logic Method of Constructing Extreme Scenarios

We demonstrate that creating objectives-focused scenarios using backwards logic can augment the conventional scenario method by enabling the creation of a broader range of scenarios than those typically constructed by the intuitive logics method. These augmented scenarios include a range of more extreme, but still plausible, scenarios that vary the achievement of extremes in the organization's over-riding objectives, whilst still preserving logical causality in scenario storylines. We demonstrate that these scenario storylines can be developed to be both engaging and plausible, yet challenging. The overall focus of our augmented approach to scenario building is, thus, to create a range of more extreme but plausible, causally-related storylines that can provoke an "organization jolt" to business-as-usual thinking.

## Chapter 9: Diagnosing Organizational Receptiveness

Our enhancements of scenario method have, in principle, the capability to provide insight and value to an organization and, as such, can aid a top management team to overcome pitfalls in decision-making. But such benefits can be attenuated by a non-receptive organizational context, as in the examples that we now set out. In two case studies, we analyze the content of the standard pre-intervention interviews using the work of Janis and Mann, who propose that high-consequence decisions with conflicted options provoke stress responses within individual decision-makers.

The level of stress is reduced by the unconscious operation of "defensive mechanisms" that maintain the decision-maker's mental equilibrium. We argue that adaptive work is needed to allow group participants to be both open about their individual viewpoints and willing to change their opinion in stressful high-consequence situations, such as those detailed in our case analyses. Successful scenario practitioners need to be able to gauge how far to challenge individual participants, both cognitively and emotionally, in the process of enabling vigilant decision-making.

# Why Should the Individual and the Organization Practice Scenario Thinking?

We see a clear need for individuals and organizations – across the private, public, non-governmental and not-for-profit sectors – to use scenario thinking. Scenario thinking offers a way for individuals and groups to face up to the threats and opportunities of the future, and their potential impact upon the organization or community. As a decision-maker in this sort of situation, you may not fully understand the complexities and ambiguities that the future may hold. In fact, you may not even think about the future, and simply continue with your present course of action.

The history of business shows that, whilst there are many companies that have achieved success over long periods from adopting a business-as-usual approach, this success has often been challenged in the longer term by new innovations and new market entrants. For example, the average life span of a Fortune 500 multinational company is between 40 and 50 years. However, one third of companies listed in the 1970 Fortune 500 had vanished by 1983 (de Geus, 1999).

Why is it that world-class companies, staffed by world-class managers, do not survive in a changing world? Why is it that others survive, but only after facing up to unanticipated threat to their dominance and seeming invincibility? IBM was, for decades, the world's leading computer manufacturer, and invented the personal computer (PC). However, it failed to exploit this new technology and product. IBM's slowness to adapt enabled, first, Compaq, then Dell, to take the lead in PC development, marketing and sales. These companies recognized the need for new business models in order to sell PCs to a new, non-traditional set of computer-users. As these companies created their own brief spell of market dominance in PCs, IBM, for a while, seemed lost. Latterly, IBM reinvented itself as a global business consultancy organization, and rebuilt its brand image and a new global success in this new form.

The threats to survival can be multiple: organizations may survive one threat only to be crippled by another that they did not see coming. Recently, the "big three" US automobile manufacturers – Chrysler, Ford and General Motors – have been amongst those worst affected by the global financial crisis. These firms dominated the US and global automotive markets for most of the twentieth century. However, their first major error was in failing to adapt to new consumer demands for smaller, more economic and more environmentally friendly vehicles in the 1980s. In that decade, Honda, Nissan and Toyota made major inroads into the US market, first through vehicle imports, then building production plants onshore. For a period in the 1990s and early 2000s, the big three avoided the impact of these demand changes by creating and living off a new craze for "sports utility vehicles". However, the unfolding financial events wiped the sheen off the gas-guzzling top end of that market and they were left exposed.

Looking further back in history, consider the example of Xerox, which in the early 1970s held a *95 percent market share* of the global copier industry. Its target customers were large corporations, and the concept of customer value was that of centrally-controlled photocopying. Xerox focused on manufacturing and leasing complex high-speed photocopiers, using its own manufacturing and sales service force to provide a complete package to those who leased its machines. Then, along came Canon – who competed head-to-head for Xerox's large corporate customer base. Why didn't Xerox appreciate the nature of the threat and respond earlier than it did to Canon's attack?

Xerox had a very strong business idea, but the very strength and invulnerability of the business idea was its undoing. Xerox was shackled with its own sales force and its leasing policy for its big machines. It could not afford to offer smaller machines to its customer base. It thought that its customers, heads of copying in large corporations, would protect both themselves *and* Xerox and retain centralized copying, since it was in both the customers' and Xerox's interests. Other parties trying the same business idea found that it could not be copied. However, individuals working in those large corporations increasingly wanted the control that the flexible and instant access to copying facilities of Canon offered.

Similarly, Motorola was unprepared for Nokia's entry into the US mobile phone market. As a first point of entry, Nokia made phones for Radio Shack, then sold its phones with a well-known carrier brand stamped on them. Nokia's basic strategy was to design phones that were user-friendly and modularized – such that even though cellular systems differ from country to country, the basic phone was almost identical, no matter where in the world it was sold. Enormous sales volumes of almost identical products allowed Nokia to reduce manufacturing overheads and unit costs.

Both Xerox and Motorola felt invulnerable – and then the worst happened: a competitor came from nowhere and established a stronghold, based on evolving customer value. Both Xerox and Motorola seem to have been unable to anticipate what would happen. Why was this? The reason is that these companies – and many others – are the prisoners of their own success. They show how, when things are running smoothly, ways of operating can become ingrained over the years.

Many organizations follow managerial recipes in a similar way to those we have mentioned, allowing their recipes to become routines that guide all thinking and actions. As writers on strategic management have argued, to survive, an organization's strategic decision-making must retain or improve the organization's alignment with the external world. In other words, recipes should not be routinely followed; rather, they should be changed altogether when appropriate and necessary. However, strategic inertia – defined as the degree of commitment to current strategy – grows over time as current ways of operating become increasingly embedded in an organization. Commitment to the status quo will tend to escalate in a smooth, undisturbed fashion, with incremental adjustments or improvements to current strategy over time. However, as highlighted, escalated commitment to business-as-usual is likely to result, at some stage, in a mismatch with changes in the business environment.

## CONSTRAINED THINKING AND THE GLOBAL FINANCIAL CRISIS OF THE 2000s

The global financial crisis and its aftermath are clear evidence of what can happen when the future is seen as a continuation of a seemingly rosy present. Just before the financial meltdown of 2008, *Business Week* published its annual survey of business forecasters and asked for their predictions on the US economy in the forthcoming year (published on December 20, 2007). The economists projected, on average, that the US economy would grow 2.1 percent from the fourth quarter of 2007 to the end of 2008. This averaged forecast was a slight down-turn from the 2.6 percent growth achieved in 2007. Only two of the 38 forecasters surveyed predicted a recession. So, economists and financial institutions in the US and across the world appear to have been totally blind to what, in hindsight, appears blindingly obvious – that lending money to those who had no immediate means or prospects of being able to repay the loans could result in a serious consequence for the US economy. The reasons that justify why the subprime lending was seen as prudent are widely known. The lending was considered "safe" because there was property as collateral. House prices had always risen in past years, and it was assumed that they would continue to rise. So, there were thought to be ever-appreciating "bricks and mortar" whose increasing value would cover the mortgagee's loan, plus interest.

We are now aware, of course, that those who did much of the lending were handing out other institutions' money and were gaining big commission payments for doing so. These lenders were exposed to no direct financial risk themselves – in technical terms, the loss function was asymmetric. The subprime mortgage debts were bundled into complex investment packages – so complex that those that bought into them did not really know what they were investing in. But, they did not seem to care. Individuals and organizations saw that their peers and competitors were entering into high-return, low-risk investments – or, so it seemed. The bonuses were huge and the lifestyle lavish. Why would any finance professional not be attracted? How could anyone resist? We are not so bold as to assert that application of scenario thinking would have avoided the global financial crisis. However, we posit that its wide use should have increased awareness of the possibility of alternative futures beyond the current trajectory, and prompted strategic planning in order to: have a broader awareness of risk, recognize the early signs of an unexpected future unfolding, be proactive in seeking to mitigate risk.

In this book, we present a clear set of guidelines and examples on "how to" undertake scenario analysis. By being aware of and practiced in the art of undertaking this type of analysis, you should be prepared to face up to the future in a proactive way. We outline how use of scenario method takes you beyond bounded thinking, and enables you to think about the future from multiple perspectives at the same time. By its very nature, scenario thinking presents an explicit challenge to "business-as-usual" thinking.

However, whilst you, as an individual, may recognize the need for adoption of a new approach to dealing with the future, we are only too aware that there are strong cultural constraints faced by those who think differently.

## SOCIETAL CONSTRAINTS ON CHALLENGE AND THE USEFULNESS OF SCENARIO THINKING

In relation to questions of why no one appeared to challenge what was happening in the cases we have outlined, we would highlight a key danger – societal pressures that stand in the way of thinking differently, thinking laterally. We live at a time when there is much talk of people being encouraged to show their individuality, to be different, to be creative. However, we would assert that the reality is very different. Ours is an age in which there are intense pressures to conform, to "go with the flow", *not* to ask questions but, instead, to comply passively with increasing regulation and control. Organizations may espouse notions of individuality but, by and large, they expect their members to be predictable corporate citizens.

Although everything from clothing to cars is marketed as enhancing the consumer's individuality, these differentiated products makes us "different" in the same way as everyone else. Democratic governments appear less and less open to question and challenge from their citizenry, the media or any other authority, even as they make decisions to go to war. At the same time, the media are less independent than in the past, more and more governed by corporate pressures and expectations. From childhood, we are encouraged to be ourselves but, at the same time, required to conform. So, how can we help individuals and organizations to challenge business-as-usual at a basic level – to challenge perceived wisdom? We offer scenario method as a mode of facilitating challenge, not through direct confrontation and opposition, but through setting alternative understandings alongside each other for reflective comparison.

Decision-makers within organizations are becoming more aware of the need to be mindful of the impact – positive or negative – of their decisions and actions, hence increasing interest in the notion of corporate social responsibility in both business school curricula and corporate reporting. The business world has begun to recognize the limitations of conventional foresight. In a 2007 *Harvard Business Review* article, Rigby and Bilodeau (2007) reported on their 14th annual survey of management tools and techniques used by 8,500 global executives. They noted that:

> in the relatively stable world of the 1990s, preparing for scenarios that had a low probability of happening ... often felt superfluous. One of the early and consistent employers of scenarios, however, was the New York Board of Trade which used what-if analyses in 1993 to decide to build a second trading floor outside the World Trade Center. That foresight kept the organization afloat after 9/11, and [it] has since created a third trading floor.

In their survey, Rigby and Bilodeau (2007) found that nearly 70% of their sample reported utilizing scenario and contingency planning in some form.

Our organizations, our technologies and our operations are more complex than they have been at any time in the past. They also take place on a much larger scale. Their effects are much greater. What we do now has impacts across the world and into the future. The issues we face and that we create for ourselves and others require new forms of joined-up thinking and analysis that take account of their complexity and trans-disciplinarity. We need to consider how we deal with business problems from the perspectives of the broadest range of stakeholders, not just our immediate employees and corporate stockholders.

Events in the Gulf of Mexico in 2010, following the Deepwater Horizon rig failure, provide a recent illustration of this. At the time of writing, this disaster was the latest in a string of business, organizational and human failures that have had broad-ranging impacts for society and the environment. Simply thinking about the range of scenarios of technological and organizational failure might not have prevented such disasters, but their possibility could have been anticipated. Those involved would then have been prepared for all possible and plausible outcomes from their core activity, and should have had a basis for risk management and contingency planning, not for what *would* happen, but for what *might* happen.

In addition to the uncertainties faced by individual organizations, we nowadays face major challenges that must be addressed at a global level, but which also have local impacts and require local responses. At a global level, we must face up to the fact that the climate is changing – climate change appears to be generally accepted, albeit that its causes and the nature and scale of its impacts remain subject to debate. At the same time, we face the realization that the world's resources are not infinite and others – including, but not restricted to the growing populations of emerging economies such as Brazil, China and India – have legitimate claims upon them. The future that the developed economies have set course towards is reliant upon access to these resources. As we write, threats around access to these resources and other global concerns persist – terrorism; pandemic, economic uncertainties. Their relative and absolute importance waxes and wanes in line with their prominence in the media and in public perception.

At the same time, we are also faced with the promise and possibility of new technologies that may help us satisfy our needs and wants. Some advocate the use of nuclear power to solve the "energy crisis", and nuclear fusion technology is fast-developing. At the same time, others are totally against the use of nuclear power and call for investment in renewable energy sources. These are developing apace, along with fuel cell and new battery technologies. Medical advances in fields including Alzheimer's disease, cancers and HIV/AIDS are being reported almost daily. New "context aware" information and communications technologies are predicted, offering both opportunities (such as constant health monitoring) and threats (such as increased surveillance and control). We could go on. Our point is that, at the very local level of the organization, region or community, various opportunities and threats will arise in the future. Our book will demonstrate that the future, whilst unpredictable, is to a large extent, knowable. Scenario thinking will help you, and your organization, to make better decisions in the face of this uncertainty.

## WHAT ARE SCENARIO THINKING AND SCENARIO METHOD?

Scenario thinking contains key components to promote the effective exchange of opinions and beliefs within a management team. The construction of multiple futures holds open airtime for differing opinions about the nature of the future, and provides a forum for the debate, questioning and synthesis of complementary, contrasting and conflicting viewpoints. Those enmeshed in particular fragments of the organization are provided with a process to achieve a synthesis of viewpoints that is likely to unite previously opposed factions. The scenario process combines space for differentiation of views with integration of different perspectives, towards a synthesis through the strategic conversation implicit in it. In this way, it assists decision-makers in steering the organization away from the excesses of group-think on the one hand, and fragmentation on the other.

The practice of scenario thinking, via the intuitive logics scenario method that we present, is a means of overcoming strategic inertia, since it implicitly accepts that managers' best guesses about the course of future events and about the appropriateness of strategic choice may be mistaken. Essentially, scenario interventions within organizations construct multiple frames of future states of the external world, only some of which may be well-aligned with current strategy. Scenario thinking can facilitate "vigilance" in strategic thinking – in that alternative futures are thought through and strategic options can subsequently be evaluated against these futures. The process of scenario thinking enhances the evaluation and integration of information, and promotes contingency planning for the unfolding of both favorable and unfavorable futures.

Multiple scenarios are pen-pictures of a range of *plausible* futures. Each individual scenario has an infinitesimal probability of actual occurrence, but the *range* of a *set* of individual scenarios can be constructed in such a way as to *frame* the uncertainties that are seen to be inherent in the future – like the edges on the boundaries surrounding a multi-dimensional space. Multiple scenarios provide alternate frames on the nature of the future. Also, and crucially, because each of the scenarios – and the space that they frame – is plausible, the events and impacts that they outline must be considered *possible* for strategic planning purposes.

It is worth comparing and contrasting scenario thinking, as described here, with planning and decision-making approaches that require judgmental forecasts and confidence assessments about the future. The judgmental process that produces such numeric forecasts is often not verbalized or recorded, so the decision-making may appear to the audience to reside within a "black box". Also, inherent in these alternative methods is the assumption that it is both useful and possible to attempt to predict the future, whereas scenario thinking assumes that the best that can be done is to identify critical future uncertainties and plan for the range of futures that could, plausibly, unfold. Essentially, scenarios highlight the reasoning underlying judgments about the future, and give explicit attention to sources of uncertainty *without* trying to turn an uncertainty into a probability.

A major focus is on *how* the future might evolve from today's point in time to the horizon year of the scenario – say 15 to 20 years hence. Scenario thinking analyses the relationships between:

- the critical *uncertainties* (as they resolve themselves);
- important predetermined *trends* (such as demographics); and
- the behavior of actors who have a stake in the particular future (who tend to act to preserve and enhance their own interests).

Because, in our approach, the scenarios are developed and produced by the key involved and affected stakeholders, the pen-pictures produced are highly plausible to them, and they are generally highly motivated to communicate them to a wider audience in the organization or community.

Alternative worldviews can be communicated easily in an organization via the medium of scenario "stories". Additionally, once a story has been read and the reasoning underlying its unfolding understood, a future has been "rehearsed". Thus, once the early events in a scenario occur, the decision-maker will be able to anticipate how the future will likely unfold. These "trigger events" will be seen as *information* among the stream of *data* that impacts upon the decision-maker. Scenario thinking can promote:

- *Early contingency action.* Just as the new purchaser of a car becomes sensitive to the variety of models of that make on the road, the scenario thinker becomes sensitive to a scenario starting to unfold and becoming reality. Such sensitivity can lead to early contingency action to counter an unfavorable future.
- *Early recognition of opportunities.* New organizational opportunities can be quickly grasped as soon as favorable scenarios begin to unfold. Such early recognition and reaction to an emerging future is seen, by some practitioners, as more useful than the creation of robust strategic options.

The typical outcomes of the scenario process include:

- Confirmation either that the overall strategy of a business is sound, or that new, underpinning strengths need to be added to create more *robustness*. (Robustness implies that a strategy performs well in each scenario.)

- Confirmation either that lower-level business choices are sound, or that new, alternative options are more robust.
- Recognition that none of the business options are robust and, therefore, contingency planning against unfavorable futures is necessary.
- Sensitivity to the "early warning" elements that are precursors of both desirable and unfavorable futures.

The scenario method contains components to promote alternative views about the nature of the future, and also challenges potentially inappropriate confidence – both in a single "best-guess" future and also in a single, tried-and-trusted strategy.

Our analytic approach is, to our minds, essential to inform and support decision-making that embraces and integrates consideration of the full set of political, economic, social, technological, ecological and legal (PESTEL) factors that will shape the future. They are wide in range, variable in their interactions, unpredictable in their outcomes, but can be explored and understood by the application of the approach known as "intuitive logics" (Jungermann and Thuring, 1987) that we introduce as you read through this text. Our structured approach to scenario thinking will enable you to:

- identify the forces in the broad business environment that are actually driving the issue forward;
- consider the range of possible and plausible outcomes of each of these forces; and
- understand how the forces interact with each other in terms of cause and effect, and chronological order;

and, from these:

- explore the "limits of possibility" for the different futures that might unfold as a result.

## OUR APPROACH

Our approach to scenario building is team-based. Those who have to make the decisions should also be those who create the scenarios.

This means that senior members of the organization – or organizations – should be intimately involved in scenario development. This group may engage an external facilitator to oversee the project but the external facilitator will simply aid the process of scenario construction, rather than add in substantive expertise on scenario content. We realize that there are limitations of this reliance on expertise that is internal within the host organization but scenario thinking is a learning experience rather than a desk-based exercise to be conducted by external experts. The true expertise lies in the heads of the individuals who are grappling with a strategic issue, rather than in the hands of external consultants.

To us, the key learning from undertaking scenario method is derived from interaction between involved actors. Each participant must engage in their own analysis of the problem, must consider what they see as the driving forces that underpin it, and must engage in considering the range of possibilities for their future impact and outcomes. More importantly, the participants must actively engage in: sharing their analysis with others, explaining their reasons for thinking as they do, and listening to and engaging with other members in order understand *their* rationale. We would immediately clarify, however, that this sharing of ideas is *not* directed at developing some shared understanding and a single viewpoint on the issue. Rather, it is about opening up strategic conversation around differences of opinion, values, beliefs and priorities. This active involvement is, to our minds, crucial to a successful outcome, whereby the involved and affected parties "own" not only the problem, but also the analytic process and the outcomes of it. In our experience, this ownership can be critical in producing an "organizational jolt" in the face of a strategically threatening scenario.

Our approach is designed to enable groups of directly involved and affected stakeholders to take individual and collective responsibility for understanding where their immediate and local concerns sit and fit within a worldview. Also, it is directed at helping the scenario team understand how their narrowly defined problem affects, and is affected by, a broad range of directly- and indirectly-related issues. Once a senior group has developed the scenarios and considered strategies against them, there is likely to be a common understanding and common purpose to subsequent actions. We believe that this level of understanding and motivation can only be achieved by a team-based exercise. Looking beyond the immediate boundaries of the involved organizational group, in Chapters 4 and 5 we present ways for the scenario team to engage critically with the longer-term implications of their decisions and actions for society and the environment, including future generations.

We recognize that there are several potential problems with the "internal expertise" mode of scenario development. First, there is obviously a major time commitment required when a group, which may consist of upwards of 20 key decision-makers, is required to commit to a scenario project. This is not just a matter of direct cost – in comparison, external consultants do not, mostly, come cheap – but, rather, of opportunity cost when senior members are taken off other projects. You need to consider this issue along with others when determining how to set up and run a scenario project.

If you are aiming to conduct a project with the sole intent of gaining a better understanding of what the problem is in order to stimulate broader thinking on it, you may opt for a one-day or 24-hour scenario workshop. This may be sufficient for your immediate purposes, or it may pave the way for further investigation using other approaches. If, however, you are exploring a very complex issue that is very much under-researched and that is of critical importance to your business, you need to consider whether the possible costs of failure to address risk are greater than the direct and opportunity costs of undertaking a full-blown scenario analysis and strategic option appraisal.

The second, and potentially more serious, problem with adopting an internal expertise approach is that of myopic or bounded thinking – that those within the problem domain will be constrained by the limitations of their contextual expertise. We discuss this issue and solutions to it in Chapters 3 and 4.

Our focus in this book is on the intuitive logics approach to scenario thinking, and we detail the core components of the technique in the next chapter. Our method leads to the creation of four plausible futures, within which the focal organization will thrive, survive, or decline. Each scenario starts at the same point in time – now. From this point, each scenario unfolds into the future by a series of causal linkages – just like a sequence of stacked dominoes falling one-by-one. In Chapter 7, we show how to evaluate the organization's current strategies against the scenarios. Is a currently-followed strategy robust against all four futures, or is it fragile, or poor-performing, against one or more of the scenarios? In Chapter 8, we evaluate further elements of an organization's preparedness in the face of inhospitable futures. All this demonstrates the implicit focus of our approach to the future – we are concerned with evaluating and improving the quality of decisions made at this point in time against a range of plausible futures. As such, our concern is with the external business environment – which is seen as uncontrollable. In short, our approach to decision-making within scenario thinking can be described as reactive.

By contrast, other approaches to scenario thinking view the decision-maker as proactive and able, to a degree, to shape the course of events. One such approach is that of "back-casting". Here, the scenario thinker constructs a scenario of a single, desirable future and then evaluates what actions need to be taken to achieve that future. Thus, the future is viewed as "masterable", rather than "dominating" (De Jouvenal, 1967). Large multinational corporations can, perhaps, influence the policies of governments and governments, of course, can set their own policies. Thus, the degree to which the focal organization possesses power – of influence or action – relates strongly to whether back-casting is a useful exercise. In our book, we focus on the smaller-scale, less powerful, organization and view the future as dominating, in de Jouvenal's terms. Nevertheless, we are concerned with the actions of the powerful, and powerless, as these actors react to the unfolding events within a particular scenario – in order to preserve and enhance their own interests.

Another approach to scenario building is to focus on the predetermined elements of the future. Such elements will, logically, be part of all scenarios. Wack (1985a, 1985b) has argued that such an emphasis in scenario-building can develop a deeper understanding of the certainties of the future than would have been salient before such consideration. Thus, scenario thinking can aid understanding of the logical, forward implications of what has already happened. Wack draws the analogy of this with the occurrence of intense rainfall near the source of the Ganges in the Himalayas, and notes that the future implications of this rainfall for towns and villages in the foothills, downstream, will be predetermined. Our book distinguishes between what are seen as predetermined elements of the future and uncertainties that can resolve themselves in ways that impact the focal organization. We focus on the causal linkages between these two sets of forces that drive the unfolding of the future.

The major inputs to our scenario method are qualitative, in that they comprise the individual interpretations of the core problem by involved and affected stakeholders. They are therefore subjective, being moderated and molded according to the beliefs and values of each participant. These inputs represent the "socially constructed reality" – or, as we will discuss in Chapter 4, "multiple realities" – of the group, rather than constituting an objective state that will be similarly read and understood by anyone else who engages with it. Whilst, from here on, we will focus on our own set of scenario approaches, we would refer the interested reader to Bradfield *et al.* (2005) and Hughes (2009), for a fuller discussion of the various "schools" of scenario thinking and how these schools emerged.

## WHAT ARE THE BUSINESS CREDENTIALS OF SCENARIO METHOD?

We are not the first or the only writers to present scenario method as a tool for strategic analysis. We cannot give a full account of its origins and development in this short text, but would offer some major sources that you may wish to follow up, and that provide further links. One of the key writers on modern business scenarios is Pierre Wack, who published two papers in the influential *Harvard Business Review* in the mid-1980s (Wack, 1985a, 1985b). Wack was one of a group of key scenario thinkers who worked with Shell during the 1980s. Another of the group who spent time at Shell was Peter Schwartz. In his book, *The Art of the Long View* (1991), Schwartz outlined the emergence of modern scenario techniques in the US military after World War II, at a time of huge "critical uncertainty" in the new era of the Cold War, the arms race to develop ever-more powerful nuclear weapons and the emergence of a new global order under two superpowers, the United States and Russia.

The Shell team also included Kees van der Heijden, author of *Scenarios: The Art of Strategic Conversation* (van der Heijden, 1996) and, in collaboration with us and others, *The Sixth Sense: Accelerating organizational learning with scenarios* (van der Heijden *et al.*, 2002). Another key writer on scenarios is Paul J.H. Schoemaker, who has published in the top-ranked *Strategic Management Journal* (Schoemaker, 1993) and has also written with Kees van der Heijden (Schoemaker and van der Heijden, 1992). We cannot list all those who have contributed to the development of scenario method as an academically rigorous mode of strategic inquiry. However, we would confirm that we have both made major contributions to the academic and practice-based literature (e.g. Cairns *et al.*, 2004, 2006, 2010; Wright *et al.*, 2004, 2008, 2009).

## CRITIQUES OF SCENARIO PLANNING AND A DEFENSE

Despite the range of authors and texts that engage with scenario method and the popularity of its use in organizations, the approach is not without its critics. Some of this criticism is directed at the term "scenario planning" – one that is frequently used, but not one that we adopt. We see *scenario thinking* as a mode of inquiry and analysis that enhances knowledge and understanding in order to inform and support planning. Scenario stories may also be used to test the robustness of plans – and strategies – against a range of futures; however, we see planning itself as a separate activity that stands alongside – but outside – scenario method.

At this point, consider the use of the term "art" in the titles of the books by Schwartz and van der Heijden referred to above. Use of this word, to our minds, provides ammunition for some critiques of scenarios, particularly from those that see managing and organizing as rational activities that are, or should be, devoid of any subjective input. These critics support a "science-based" approach to management and organization studies. However, we would argue that an exclusively science-based perspective on strategic analysis is, in itself, fragile and bounded in its rationality. We see it as naïve and simplistic, as well as flying in the face of all evidence, to think that management and organization can ever be activities that are *not* influenced and impacted by subjectivity, and individual beliefs and values. Scenario thinking is definitely an "art" form, and must be recognized and valued as such. Even so, the method also allows space for consideration of fact and data based upon rational and objective analysis.

We do not consider that the pairs of terms subjectivity/objectivity and rationality/emotionality are mutually exclusive. Rather, we see scenario thinking as a creative process that involves subjectivity, intuition and emotion, but which *also* involves rationality and objectivity. In engaging with the method, we advocate that all information, ideas and opinions put forward in a scenario development exercise should be embraced and then, crucially, evaluated for relevance and usefulness in the creation of plausible scenarios of the future.

Some writers (e.g. Hodgkinson, 2001; Hodgkinson and Sparrow, 2002) have criticized scenario planning as being a "practitioner tool" with little theoretical underpinning, or an "imperfect tool" (e.g. Hamel, 2000; Hyde, 1999; Mintzberg, 1994; Mintzberg *et al.*, 1998; Porter, 1985). These critics say that scenario stories offer mere speculation on the nature of the future, dealing with matters of opinion rather than fact. In fact, early scenario practitioners did develop scenarios whilst offering little in the way of explanation of how they have arrived at these particular scenarios, rather than any others. Such practices were poorly conceived, unfortunately, leading critics such as Mintzberg *et al.* (1998) to question the amount of time expended on scenarios for little apparent output. Similarly, Porter (1985) questioned how managers might be expected to respond to matters of speculation, rather than fact. Notably, Mintzberg (1994: 248) has criticized scenarios as offering a scattergun approach to investigation of the future, in that "by speculating upon a variety (of futures), you might just hit upon the right one". As we shall set out in this book, scenario thinking using the intuitive logics method is a systematic way of looking into the future, and one that is focused on perceptions of the causal unfolding of events. As such, scenario thinking has a strong basis centered on providing an explanation of the course of future events. Present day scenario thinking is neither speculation nor scattergun prediction.

To address the limitations of an exclusively art- or science-based approach, we present scenario thinking as an approach that integrates aspects of both. In doing this, we posit that it provides structure to intuitive thought, a framework for incorporating rational thought, and support for challenge to initial intuitions – such that higher-level intuition is developed. We also recognize that strategic thinking, analysis and decision-making are moderated by the "social construction of reality" (Berger and Luckmann, 1966), and that issues of power and influence are central in determining how situations will unfold. In this recognition, we align with Flyvbjerg (1998) and others who argue that power is a key determinant of political, organizational and economic thinking, and that rationalization, rather than rationality, is central to decision-making.

As we shall see, stakeholder analysis – a component of the intuitive logics approach to scenario development – allows the scenario thinker to understand the role of power, and the powerful, in determining the unfolding of the future ... and who wins and loses as a result.

Throughout the rest of this book, we will develop discussion of scenario thinking and scenario method. We will explain how you can expand the range of your thinking in order to accommodate options and uncertainties. We will show you how to apply the method, with explanations of why each stage is undertaken, and what outcomes should come from it. We do not prescribe a single way in which to operate. Rather, we present a "menu" of options for the method. You will chose which stages to use and which to omit – based upon your own context, the issues that you are addressing, the people with whom you are working, and the time and other resources at your disposal.

# Working with Scenarios: Introducing the Basic Method

In this chapter, we set out the various stages of the basic scenario process. This model follows the approach developed over many decades by a number of writers (e.g. Schwartz, 1991; van der Heijden *et al.*, 2002) and organizations (e.g. Global Business Networks (GBN); SRI International). As outlined in Chapter 1, it relies upon the application of "intuitive logics" (Jungermann and Thuring, 1987), and is focused on the development of multiple scenarios that explore the "limits of possibility" for the future, rather than on the development of singular, "normative" scenarios of some ideal future to which to aspire. We have worked with and developed this scenario method over many years, engaging with many different organizational and country contexts, and with a variety of mixes of stakeholders. We have operated within project timescales that range from a few hours and a single set of rough scenarios, to several months and multiple iterations of scenario development, leading to highly-detailed scenario presentations. In order to enable you to develop and apply your own skills in working with scenarios in different situations, we offer approaches to creating scenarios that range from the application of "scenario thinking" by the individual in analyzing options in response to a complex problem within a constrained timeframe, to the use of "scenario method" by groups of diverse organizational members and stakeholders working together over a period of a few hours or many months. We outline the various stages of our scenario method, each of which addresses a specific element of the analytic process. At this point, we must clarify that, in our experience, having a fairly tightly structured process makes it easier and more comfortable for participants to deal with the complexities, ambiguities and uncertainties of the content. The rigid structure provides a lifeline within the sea of turbulence.

The initial approaches to scenario development that we outline have the common feature of enabling individuals and groups to explore the limits of possibility for the unfolding of the issue under consideration over a specified timescale, within the confines of what is currently known, knowable and plausible. Whilst this approach will broaden the range of thinking beyond business-as-usual, the limits of possibility and plausibility that participants perceive may remain bounded. In Chapter 3, we explain some of the reasons for this, and offer some techniques for overcoming this limitation. Thereafter, in Chapters 4 and 5 we introduce and illustrate augmented scenario methods. The first of these is based upon deeper analysis, exploring individual "driving forces" in greater detail. The second involves broader engagement outside the organizational context, enabling and supporting development of scenarios that address the concerns of stakeholders beyond those with immediate involvement and interest. The latter approach is intended to expand your thinking to consider alternative social, organizational and environmental contexts.

In Chapter 8, we introduce scenario approaches that challenge the notion that the future will be incremental, with consideration of transformational approaches. We prompt thinking on "step change" future possibilities, where the steps may be fairly manageable or, alternatively, daunting. Manageable steps are likened to mild earth tremors, where pressure in the "tectonic" system builds up unnoticed until there is a sudden change – perhaps frightening, but not fatal. After the event, things have moved. The constituent parts remain the same, but there is a noticeable shift that requires some adaptation. However, with daunting steps, we outline alternative scenario approaches that are based upon "magnitude 7+" systemic upheaval – "disaster" scenarios. These start by assuming some future dramatic, but plausible event that causes major disruption to the present state. However, we must stress that the dramatic events we are dealing with here do not lack causality. We are not dealing with issues of the type, "Martians have landed – what should we do?" The end state of the big shift is explored and explained by application of "backwards logic", in order to describe the route from end state to present through "effect–cause" reasoning. Finally, in providing a full set of "scenario tools", we show how scenario method can be applied in thinking not only of the impact of events upon those stakeholders with a direct involvement and interest – those who can directly affect the situation or are immediately involved, but also upon the broader range of societal stakeholders who may be affected by decisions and actions, both now and in the future.

But that is for later. For the present, however, back to the basic approach.

This chapter is set out as follows. First, we provide a light-hearted example of how we believe all human beings are natural scenario thinkers, and show that scenario method is not something complex and inaccessible to the layperson. Second, we explain and illustrate in detail the particular scenario method that forms the foundation for later advancement within this book. We set out the full list of "ingredients" of scenario method as a set of detailed process stages to be undertaken sequentially. In this chapter, there is a "set menu". However, in the later chapters, we add new options and outline a sequence of stages that is variable. Specifically, in Chapter 5, we present two "augmented" methods that build upon the basic method in order to add further detail to the analysis. In later chapters, we also show how and why the stages may be undertaken in different orders, and how some stages may be curtailed or omitted, according to needs and resources. We explain the reasons for, and the risks and benefits of, different option selections. We also discuss the ways in which different scenario approaches might be applied within different problem contexts. We include illustrative examples of how these selections operate in practice, and we evaluate the advantages and disadvantages of each of the scenario approaches.

Throughout this chapter, we provide illustrative diagrams to show the *format* of the outputs from the various stages of the basic scenario process, and short examples to explain what is expected in *content* terms as the outcome. As we have outlined, actual implementation of the method may take place across a range of timescales, from one day to several iterations over months. In the Appendix, we provide a one-page timetable for "24-hour scenarios" with which you can work. This is a model that we have applied with success on numerous occasions. The 24-hour model is preferable to a "one-day" scenario approach, in that it offers an evening in which participants can discuss their emerging under-standings, question one another, and raise new lines of inquiry for the next day. It also allows them to "sleep on it", although experi-ence shows that this often leads to people wakening very early the next day with some "aha!" thought that brings a new bearing on the problem at hand.

Whichever approach you adopt to group scenario building, we provide a set of basic ground rules that should be followed in every case. These set the context for challenge to business-as-usual thinking, support inclusiveness and the expression of multiple viewpoints on the matter at hand, and minimize the risk of inter-personal challenge and conflict between participants. If these ground rules are not followed, there is a serious risk of breakdown of the process, with some individuals becoming alienated and excluded, and powerful actors dominating and closing down the discussion.

## SCENARIO THINKING AS A WAY OF BEING

Before we launch into the detail of a structured scenario method, we wish to debunk any myth that scenarios are something special, or a novel way for people to address uncertainties. Our view is that human beings are *natural* scenario thinkers. We do not see scenario thinking as some intricate process that is the reserved domain of the "expert" or the "scenario planner". Despite our presentation of the theoretical and philosophical bases of our approach, we see it as something fundamentally quite simple. You don't believe us?

Imagine that you have been invited to attend a job interview. You really want this job. You are sitting outside the interview room, but you have been given no indication of who you are about to face. Unless you are extremely stupid, or pompously over-confident, you will be creating scenarios in your mind. How many people will be on the interview panel? Will the setting be formal or informal? Will they be relaxed and friendly, or detached and interrogative? What questions will they ask me? What if they ask about this, or about that? The list goes on. If you are a fairly normal, fairly sensi-ble human being, you will be running through various "scenarios" of how the future might unfold. It is likely that none of them will come true as "the future", but also likely that elements of some or all of them *will* come true.

It is this form of "intuitive logics" that we apply in what you are about to read. It is not rocket science!

## ELEMENTS OF OUR FOCAL SCENARIO METHOD

The following is a list of the main stages into which we sub-divide the basic scenario process.

## The scenario process in action

Stage 1: *Setting the Agenda* – defining the issue and process, and setting the scenario timescale

Stage 2: *Determining the Driving Forces* – working, first, individually, and then as a group

Stage 3: *Clustering the Driving Forces* – group discussion to develop, test and name the clusters

Stage 4: *Defining the Cluster Outcomes* – defining two extreme, but yet highly plausible – and hence, possible – outcomes for each of the clusters over the scenario timescale

Stage 5: *Impact/Uncertainty Matrix* – determining the key scenario factors, A and B

Stage 6: Framing the Scenarios – defining the extreme outcomes of the key factors, A1/A2 and B1/B2

Stage 7: *Scoping the Scenarios* – building the set of broad descriptors for four scenarios

Stage 8: *Developing the Scenarios* – working in sub-groups to develop scenario storylines, including key events, their chronological structure, and the "who and why" of what happens.

Having provided this overall list of the stages, we now explain in detail what is involved in undertaking the process. We tell you what resources are required or recommended, how to manage the process, and how to instruct participants in what is expected of them and what they will learn from doing it. As you read through the various chapters and sections that outline the basic method, augmented methods and alternative approaches, we offer comment and examples to guide your thinking on how to select the most appropriate scenario approach for your particular project implementation needs, related to:

- the nature of the problem being addressed (degree of uncertainty, complexity, impact);
- the timescale in which the project is to be undertaken;
- the resources available for undertaking the project (time, people, funding);
- the degree to which it addresses stakeholder interests (directly involved/affected, third parties, future generations); and

- the output that is expected from the project by its key sponsors (clearer understanding of the problem, a framework for option appraisal, a model for strategic planning support).

## GENERAL INTRODUCTION AND PREPARATION

Scenario method offers *one* approach to understanding and analyzing seemingly intractable problems where there are "critical uncertainties" that span a range of subject areas or disciplinary boundaries. It is an approach that is inclusive, rather than selective. As such, it can be used in conjunction with, can incorporate information and data from, and can provide input to, other methods. It can be used by individuals, but is particularly suited to groups with different organizational, social and disciplinary backgrounds.

Relying upon the approach of "intuitive logics", groups make sense of the issue by using all available sources, including quantitative and qualitative research data, published reports, media outputs, and so on – any material that is relevant and informs thinking. Scenario method is a democratic process where all viewpoints are considered equal, and all ideas can be aired and discussed using an open and non-confrontational approach. In it, we do not consider the degree of probability of whether or not any event *will* happen, only its plausibility and the possibility that it *could* happen.

Throughout the following sections, you will find that we refer to the use of paper-based resources, including sticky notes, flip charts, large sheets of paper, and the like. We are aware that the exercise can be designed around and undertaken using computers and a range of software options that enable participants to share ideas and interact electronically. However, having worked with both approaches, we consider that the types of strategic conversation, in-depth probing and questioning of ideas and concepts, and the non-adversarial creative conflict that the process is intended to nurture, are much more freely generated and actively supported using low-tech materials.

Scenario method does not provide "the answer" to the problem. Scenario stories themselves are *not* predictions of the future. Rather, they offer a range of future possibilities against which to test current plans, to develop and appraise new options and, hopefully, to make better-informed and more robust decisions on action. Scenarios provide a means of better understanding the complexity and ambiguity of the present.

## Guiding principles

We have developed the following guiding principles from our experience in facilitating a wide range of scenario projects in the UK, Europe, Asia and Australia. These have involved working with single firms, and with groups of individuals or organizations with diverse interests. We have engaged with groups of from five to over 35 participants. In addition, the projects have run over timescales that range from one day to ten weeks. Whatever the scale or context of the project, these principles can – and, in our view, should – be known and held to by all participants.

1.   The scenario process is one of creative thinking where the aim is to open up consideration of all possibilities in a complex and ambiguous world, not to close down thinking through selectivity and exclusion.

2.   Whilst the process is one of innovative and creative thinking, we prescribe a very structured approach set out in clear "stages". This structure is designed to avoid either a decline into chaos or domination by powerful individuals, with the result that some members may be marginalized or drop out. It should be followed with some degree of rigor.

3.   However, the structure should be seen as providing guidelines rather than being prescriptive, so it can be flexibly adapted to suit specific needs.

4.   At any stage in the process, new ideas can be added. This is particularly relevant at the later stages (Stage 6 onwards), when it might be thought that only those ideas that have emerged at the earlier stages can be allowed to enter the scenario stories.

5.   Keep an open mind to all possibilities, and be willing to challenge your own "business-as-usual" thinking.

## Ground rules

The following ground rules *must* be agreed by team members, and adhered to at all times:

1.   When discussing issues as a group, use a "round robin" approach, where each member gets to express her/his opinion

in turn, working clockwise around the group and starting with a different person at each issue.

*Note: If the person sitting in the opening position of a clockwise order happens to be a dominant individual with set opinions, start at the other end and run anti-clockwise!*

2. As opinions are expressed, allow only questions of clarification, such as "Why do you think that ...?", "What would happen if ...?", "Who do you think would ...?"

3. Accept that the outcome of the round robin may be consensus, majority/minority viewpoints, or complete fragmentation. Conflict of ideas is to be encouraged.

4. Take note of all generated viewpoints and build them into your consideration of the broadest range of possibilities.

5. Throughout the process, do not allow any idea to be challenged or excluded on the basis that it is "wrong" or "nonsense", unless it can be proved so without doubt and with *everyone's* agreement.

6. Roles should be allocated at the outset as necessary. As a minimum, groups should agree a Chair to guide the process, an assertive Timekeeper to keep it flowing in accordance with the agreed timetable, and a Scribe to take notes and keep control of the paperwork.

Experience has shown that the best learning approach to scenario method is through active participation. Our role – whether in MBA teaching, scenario training, or in consultancy projects – is that of process facilitators, not as content providers. The participants are always the focus of content generation and context expertise – so, it is *the participants'* thinking and analysis that determines the end result, *not* that of the facilitators.

## Preparation

Before coming to any scenario workshop, participants should be asked to undertake some initial reading on the issue that will form the focus of the event. How this is structured and directed will vary considerably, depending upon the type of scenario project and its timescale. At a basic level, if you are running a one-day scenario project in order to explore the "limits of possibility" for a predetermined uncertainty of which all are aware, you can ask participants to do homework on it, or you can direct them to specific readings.

If, however, you are setting up a complex project that involves a wide range of stakeholders who are not yet agreed on the key focal issue of concern – beyond knowing that there is something crucial that they don't currently know – you will need to set up some more in-depth prior investigation. We suggest that this is best done through following the process set out in Stage 1 (p. 29).

If you are following this approach, you should identify the broadest range of key decision-making, power-holding and directly-affected stakeholders, and arrange to conduct a series of semi-structured interviews with them. Semi-structured interviews allow interviewees to express their own views about what is important and how they feel about these matters, but offers some direction towards what is necessary to inform a scenario project. The use of a set of interviews also allows consideration of the degree of convergence/ divergence that exists amongst key decision-makers in relation to specific issues. The degree of such agreement or diversity can provide early indication as to whether such issues are largely predetermined in terms of outcomes, or represent critical uncertainties. Since scenarios are concerned with exploring the future in order to inform the present, we generally adopt the question structure set out in Stage 1 in order to guide the interview process.

Having collated and transcribed the individual interviews (these can be either from voice recordings or from written notes), we undertake "content analysis".

*Note: The latter would need to be checked and confirmed by the interviewee, once transcribed.*

Content analysis involves reading and re-reading the interviews in order to identify relevant *issues* being raised and discussed. With many hundreds of statements and a wide range of issues identified, we group the issues to identify a smaller range of higher-level *themes* that encapsulate sets of issues. For example, within a theme of "management structures", there may well be a range of more specific issues that emerge in relation to matters such as power, hierarchy, inclusion/exclusion, openness/detachment, and so on. The range of overarching themes might, for example, relate to management or political structures, to economic conditions, to social relationships, to geographic or climatic conditions. The key element of content analysis is that the issues and themes emerge from the interview content and what the interviewees have found important, not from the reader's mind and what she/he thinks *should* be important. From this content analysis, a report is compiled in which all statements are included under these emergent theme/issue titles, and where none are attributed to individuals.

Once the process of content analysis is completed – which may involve several iterations of reading and "coding" (identifying themes and issues), with changes of themes and refinement of their content – the interview content can be restructured into a project report. This report presents all of the interview statements, but set out under the theme and issue headings and without attribution to the individual who originally made each comment.

*Note: Editing may be required to remove names within a quotation, or text that links a contentious statement back to an identifiable source. Any such editing should be minimal and must not change the meaning.*

This may appear a lengthy and resource-intensive process. However, we would say that it is invaluable in setting the scene for a scenario project involving diverse, and possibly conflicting, stakeholder concerns. The report provides background reading that enables project participants to gain an overview and under-standing of the broad range of views and opinions held about the context of the project. Frequently, it raises awareness in individuals of viewpoints to which they were previously oblivious.

Whether you are leading a simple or a complex scenario proj-ect, we advise that you should direct participants' initial thinking about the issue, asking them to consider what *they* see as the driv-ing forces – political, economic, social, technological, ecological and legal (PESTEL) factors – that will impact it over the coming years. Identifying the greatest possible range of driving forces forms the starting point for our exploration. Participants should be asked to bring with them any notes they prepare, key documents that they have read, press cuttings they consider of interest, and so on for use and reference during the workshop.

## Organizing a Scenario Process Workbook

Since scenario projects are participatory – and, in our view, demo-cratic and engaging – we suggest that every participant should have reference documentation that enables her/him to follow the process. In many projects, we have constructed, printed and distributed a Scenario Process Workbook, which is issued to every participant in advance of the event and which they are required to bring to the workshop. Not only does this enable them to follow the process, stage by stage, it allows them to be aware in advance of what the full process is, what each stage involves and, hopefully, to understand why early stages may appear to be restrictive and directive, not allowing the type of creative thinking that we advocate.

## For the future

The scenario approach that we outline in this chapter is designed to enable groups of individuals to engage in structured analysis and consideration of a complex issue over time – whether one day or six months. It involves a number of stages that may appear, individually, time-consuming and resource-intensive. However, scenario thinking as an approach can be used in relation to any and every problem. We urge you to seek to develop a way of being in which, if you are given half an hour to come up with the answer to a problem, you do not immediately look for "the answer". Rather, we urge you to start by thinking through the possible futures in which the outcome will be enacted, then to consider options for action against these futures. Then, and only then, posit a solution that offers either the "right" answer for any future, the "best" answer for the range of possible futures, or the "set" of answers to cover any likelihood.

## THE SCENARIO PROCESS IN ACTION

This section is designed to enable you to facilitate and give direction to a live scenario project. It is written in a style that is intended both to brief you in advance on the content, process and intended outcome of each state, and to allow you to read it to or with participants in a project in real time in order to keep the process moving.

## Stage 1: Setting the scenario agenda

Scenario method is used to analyze and make sense of the broad "business environment" in which the issue is situated – the PESTEL context. It explores the range of possible and plausible futures that might unfold, and in which the key issue will evolve in response to both the external environment and the different strategies and actions by stakeholders.

The first stage in the process is to determine the **key focal issue** about the future faced by the group/organization/community.

---

**Example 2.1: two exemplar focal issues**

1  In this exercise, you will be exploring the potential of social network-ing sites as enablers of community engagement in political process at the local government level in West County.
2  This project will explore the viability of the company over the next 10 to 20 years – will it survive and thrive, or decay and decline?

---

Having determined the focal issue, you then decide upon an appropriate future time frame within which to work. This should not extend so far into the future as to require "science fiction" thinking, or be so close that the future is fairly predictable. It should represent a reasonable long-term planning horizon in rela-tion to the business issue.

*Note: This time frame varies. For the computer software industry, the time horizon is likely to fairly close. In considering future care needs for the elderly, it is likely to be much further ahead.*

In projects involving large organizations or groups of organiza-tions where there is a range of uncertainties about how the future might unfold, it is common to start the whole process with a series of semi-structured interviews, as outlined in the section on preparation (p. 26). Interviews are held with a range of involved and affected stakeholders, in order to gain a broad understanding of the context in which the issue sits. The interviews are loosely structured around an agenda that starts with individuals' personal ideas about an ideal future, comes back to consideration of the present and, finally, probes ideas about how history has brought the group to where they now stand. Questions might include:

1  How would you, personally, like to be able to describe an ideal future for the (organization/group/region/city) in (two/five/ten) years' time?
2  What do you think will be the key factors and events that will be necessary to make this happen?
3  Who do you think will be the key players in making this happen?

4    What factors at the present time do you see as forming founda-
     tions for the ideal future?
5    What obstacles do you see in the present that might prevent
     this future happening?
6    What do you think have been the main factors over the past
     five years in bringing us to where we are now?

From these interviews, we undertake the content analysis
process, to identify the common themes and issues in order to
compile a project briefing report. In presenting the content of different interviews under the headings of common themes and issues,
the report will also show up differences in opinion about how
these issues are perceived by different stakeholders. In Chapter 4,
we will discuss how "reality" is subject to different interpretations
by different groups and individuals. The interview report forms the
agenda for the first stage of working, where the group identifies the
key issue around which the scenarios are developed. The report
also sensitizes participants to consider the full range of driving
forces that might impact the key focal issue – to think beyond their
own immediate context of operation, and to consider whether these
forces point towards predetermined outcomes, or to uncertainties
for further consideration.

## Stage 2: Determining the driving forces – working individually then as a group

Driving forces are:

> "Those fundamental forces that bring about change or move-
> ment in the patterns and trends that we identify as under-
> pinning observable events in the world. Understanding of the
> inter-relatedness of these forces will provide insight into the
> systemic structure of the problem that we are exploring." (van
> der Heijden *et al.*, 2002: 282).

Here, we must stress that the driving forces we are considering are
those in the organization's contextual environment – not its own
internal world. They are, by and large, outside the organization's
direct control, and concern the macro-economic, the geopolitical,
constitutional and other higher-level drivers. At the detailed level,
to which we will point you below (p. 31), individual driving forces

may bring in some element of the stakeholder environment and action, but the focus must always be on external cause/internal effect relationships, not internal action/external impact. The latter is a matter of organizational strategic and operational response to the contextual environment – a matter to which we will return in later chapters.

The process of identifying driving forces is conducted, first, on an individual basis, to elicit multiple perspectives on the focal issue and to ensure that they are recorded and presented as such. In order to do this, it helps to encourage thinking in terms of the broad PESTEL framework. The PESTEL headings are, however, mere topics and, as such, they do not constitute driving forces by themselves.

*Note: MBA students frequently start off scenario construction by listing simple topics rather than forces.*

Driving forces should be defined in as few words as possible, but sufficient to make them understandable to everyone without further explanation. Driving forces are distinguished from "subjects", "topics" or "events" by pointing to an outcome. Driving force terminology might usefully include terms like "Outcome of…", "Extent of…", "Changing attitudes to…", "Number of…", and so on. However, the terminology used should never assume a particular outcome (e.g. "Increase in…") unless that direction of change is inevitable (i.e. there is no possibility of "Decrease in…"). You are encouraged to think broadly to identify the range of driving forces, whilst thinking very specifically and with focus to define individual driving forces.

Every driving force must be recorded on an individual sticky note.

*Note: Once the group has collated all its driving force notes, they should be coded numerically, 1, 2, 3 … 123 etc.*

Figure 2.1 shows representative examples of some driving forces from the first project in Example 2.1 above, exploring the potential of social networking sites as enablers of community engagement in political process at the local government level.

In large, complex projects, the stage of individual noting of driving forces should not be time constrained. In addition, if the lead-in to a project enables it to happen, it is useful to encourage participants to think of driving forces in advance of the event, and to bring notes on these with them. In shorter projects, however, it may be necessary to set a limit of about 15 minutes. In either

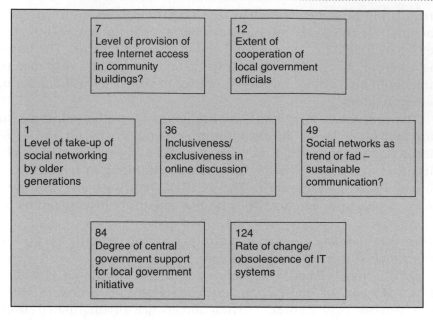

**Figure 2.1** Representative "driving force" presentations

case, participants should be asked to define the forces in fairly simple terms, focused on individual issues and indicating a point of impact relevant to the focal issue.

---

**Example 2.2**

"Inflation" is *not* a valid economic driving force for two reasons. First, it is merely a topic, with no indication of impact on the focal issue. Second, it is a value-laden topic, precluding the possibility of *deflation*.

- For a UK manufacturer, an economic driving force might be: "Impact of UK economic conditions on exports to Eurozone";
- For an Australian resources firm, it might be "Impact of a mining tax on competitiveness with Canadian extraction firms".

These both refer to a specific issue and a particular point of impact, but without prejudging what the impact will be.

---

After individuals have completed their identification of driving forces, use a round robin approach to go through them all as a group, to clarify wording and meaning.

*Note: At this stage, it is only required that there should be agreement on the meaning of the terminology used, not on the nature and impact of the force defined.*

## Stage 3: Clustering the driving forces

According to psychologists, at any given time the human brain can comfortably make sense of a maximum of about a dozen concepts in relation to each other. In large scenario projects, hundreds of driving forces may be generated! How do we make sense of this mass of ideas? One option is to jump to making decisions about "what is important". In scenario thinking, this is seen as risking the exclusion of possible interaction effects between driving forces.

The approach taken here is that of **clustering** – holding a group conversation about how the driving forces relate to one another in one of two ways: cause/effect and chronology.

### *Cause/effect*

This is the emergence of the outcome of one driving force that will have a direct impact on the outcome of another.

---

**Example 2.3**

It might be reasonably assumed that the outcome of a driving force of "Effectiveness of Internet security for online banking" will have some impact on one that posits "Extent of cyber-fraud in retail banking". This might, in turn, impact one on "Degree of customer confidence in Internet banking".

---

### *Chronology*

This is the outcome of one driving force that is dependent upon the prior reconciliation of another.

---

**Example 2.4**

The outcome of a driving force on "Changing focus of US carbon-pricing policy" will likely be influenced over, say, a 10-year time horizon by driving forces relating to the outcome of presidential elections that *will* take place in November 2012 and November 2016.

---

The aim of the clustering exercise is to find one set of linkages (out of an indefinite number of possibilities) to identify a smaller number (around 10–12 maximum) of **higher-level factors** that *directly affect the focal issue*. Figure 2.2 indicates what a completed cluster diagram might typically look like from a scenario project on futures of urban transport networks. This cluster addresses possible levels of growth in inner city housing, which relates to intensification of land use and will compare with suburban development and increasing urban sprawl.

Once the driving forces are clustered, the logic of the clusters is tested in two ways:

- by drawing linkages of cause/effect and chronology between the elements within each cluster, so that every component driving force is linked in some way to every other driving force,

and

- by "naming" the cluster in terms of the higher-level factor, then checking that every driving force is relevant to this factor.

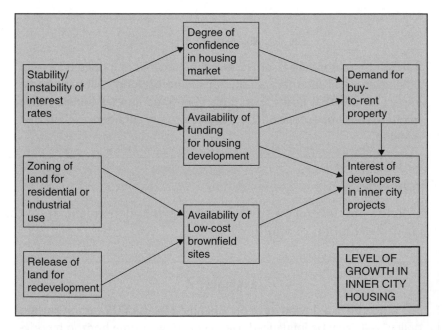

**Figure 2.2** Representative "cluster" model

*Note: If any driving force is not encapsulated by the selected name, either revisit the name, or check to which other cluster the driving force does relate.*

It should be noted that there may be a single driving force that does not fit within any of the named clusters. It is perfectly justifiable to have a "cluster" of one.

Once the group is satisfied with the clustering, the "names" should be added for record purposes, using sticky notes and identifying the name by use of capital letters or some color coding (see Figure 2.2). *Note: Duplicate "name" sticky notes should also be prepared for use in Stage 5, whilst the cluster information is held as a unit.*

## Stage 4: Defining the cluster outcomes

For each cluster, the group debates and discusses the range of possible **extreme outcomes** that might arise from it over the scenario time scale – say, between 7 and 10 years. From this, the group identifies two extreme, but very plausible – and, hence, very possible – outcomes. However, as with individual driving forces, they may be very complex in their make-up and it may not be possible to define them along a single continuum. It may be helpful to think of the extreme outcomes like two of many lines of dominoes, stacked to run out from the "epicentre" of the cluster. They may not run straight, possibly not in opposite directions to each other, but when – not if – the dominoes fall, these two sets will create the greatest impact on their surroundings.

The group should brainstorm short descriptions of how they envisage the extreme outcomes of each cluster (i.e. higher-level factor), again thinking of extremes that are both possible and plausible   scenario method in the form used here does not engage with implausible extremes beyond what is knowable within the scenario time frame, i.e. sequences of events that have no causal links to the present day.

In considering the extreme outcomes of each factor, do not confine thinking only to descriptors that are directly related to that factor – for example, the outcomes of the individual driving forces within it. Rather, at this point develop thinking on impacts across other fields to start to explore and understand the inherent cause-and-effect linkages that exist between them.

---

**Example 2.5**

Consider how structural failure in the US subprime mortgage market had rolling impacts: first, on banks across the US, Europe and other areas; then on broader financial markets – affecting investment fund availability and investor confidence; and, ultimately, country economies and the entire global financial system.

---

The set of outcomes for each factor should be recorded on flip chart sheets, or large sheets of paper. Figure 2.3 shows an example of the types of notes that might be generated, bearing in mind that we are dealing with issues of plausibility and possibility within the scenario time scale – not with an "ideal world" view. Once you have completed the individual sheets for each factor, lay these aside for later use in Stages 6 and 7, and return to using only the factor "name" sticky notes for Stage 5.

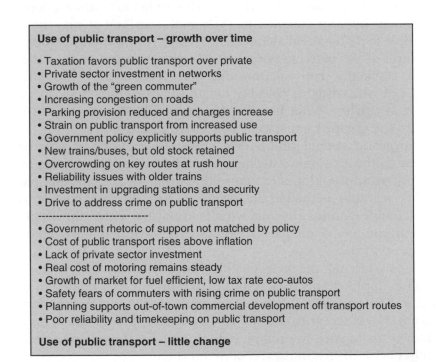

**Use of public transport – growth over time**

• Taxation favors public transport over private
• Private sector investment in networks
• Growth of the "green commuter"
• Increasing congestion on roads
• Parking provision reduced and charges increase
• Strain on public transport from increased use
• Government policy explicitly supports public transport
• New trains/buses, but old stock retained
• Overcrowding on key routes at rush hour
• Reliability issues with older trains
• Investment in upgrading stations and security
• Drive to address crime on public transport
--------------------------------
• Government rhetoric of support not matched by policy
• Cost of public transport rises above inflation
• Lack of private sector investment
• Real cost of motoring remains steady
• Growth of market for fuel efficient, low tax rate eco-autos
• Safety fears of commuters with rising crime on public transport
• Planning supports out-of-town commercial development off transport routes
• Poor reliability and timekeeping on public transport

**Use of public transport – little change**

**Figure 2.3** Representative "Extreme outcomes" record

## Stage 5: Impact/uncertainty matrix

Having determined the higher-level factors, we now move towards a framework for construction of the scenario stories. This framework is structured around **two key factors** (Factor A and Factor B). In order to identify these key factors, we first draw a matrix with two axes (see Figures 2.4 and 2.5), with which we work sequentially.

### *Horizontal axis: High/low impact*

First, we consider the **relative degree of impact** of each of the factors *on the focal issue* over the project time scale. This is done through a critically discursive debate on the range of possible events and impacts that each might generate, and the relative significance of these in determining the overall focal issue outturn. We place the factor name sticky notes along the full length of this axis by a process of negotiation and debate (see Figure 2.4).

### *Vertical axis: High/low uncertainty*

Once we have completed placement of the sticky notes – and *not before* – we consider the **relative degree of uncertainty** about their impact *on the focal issue* over the project time scale. Here, we must be absolutely clear that we are *not* discussing certainty/

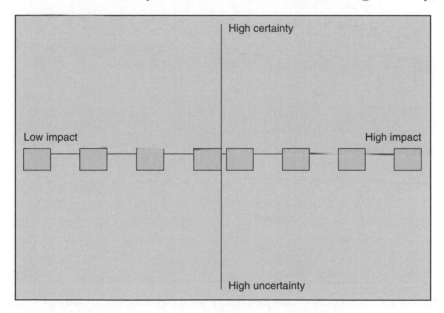

**Figure 2.4** Impact/uncertainty matrix: relative impact of factors

uncertainty about *whether* there will be an impact, but about *what* that impact may be.

---

**Example 2.6**

We may be considering a factor that we are absolutely certain will occur, such as "Impact of climate change", on the basis that there does seem to be consensus that the Earth's climate *is* changing. However, we may remain very uncertain about the actual outcomes. At present, there remains a wide discrepancy in the views of different scientific and political bodies as to both the cause of change and the possible extent of its impacts.

In this example, the factor "Impact of climate change" would likely be rated as a "high uncertainty" factor due to the differences in opinion on the possible *outcomes* of change, despite any consensus on the *existence* of change.

---

*Note: The movement of factors on the uncertainty axis should be done without disturbing their position on the impact axis, but with them ranged along the full length of the axis (see Figure 2.5).*

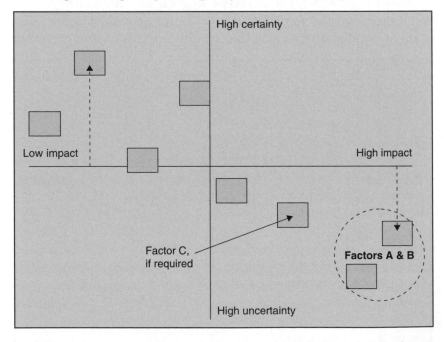

**Figure 2.5** Impact/uncertainty matrix: relative certainty/uncertainty of outcomes

Factors A and B are the two higher-level factors that are considered to combine the highest impact on the focal issue with the greatest uncertainty about what that impact may be. A crucial step is to test whether the two factors that have been selected are independent of one another. To do this, consider the resolution of the contents of Factor A as outcome A1, and the resolution of the contents of Factor B as outcome B1. Could A1 and B1 plausibly co-exist in the same future? If so, consider A1 and B2, and ask the same question. Next, consider A2 and B1 and then A2 and B2. If all four combinations are plausible, Factor A and Factor B are viewed as independent of one another, and it will be possible to develop four scenarios. If one or more of the four combinations is viewed by the scenario team as implausible, then Factors A and B are not independent of one another. At this point, Factors A and B could be combined as one factor and another possible factor, Factor C , should be selected as a potential second factor from the previously developed impact/predictability matrix.

---

**Example 2.7**

In the example of the scenario project on urban transport networks (p. 34), it is likely that outcomes of a cluster on "Policy decisions on road vs. rail networks" will be intrinsically linked to those for one on "Level of investment in suburban rail network". On the other hand, the outcomes of a cluster on "Public demand for suburban rail travel" will not necessarily be closely linked to levels of investment.

---

You should note here that, whilst other decision analysis tools might draw upon probability analysis or similar in order to make choices about what is *most likely* to happen, scenario method moves forward without such probability assessments. Rather, it maintains consideration only of everything that might feasibly happen, and prepares us for any eventuality. Any use of probability analysis should follow completion of the scenario program, as a separate exercise.

## Stage 6: Framing the scenarios

Whilst each of the higher-level factors from Stage 3 is seen to be impacting upon the focal issue and having an influence on its future outturn, the nature of its outcome is likely to vary across different future scenarios. At this point, we return to consideration of the extreme outcomes of the various factors that we outlined in Stage 4. We discuss the range of outcomes from all the factors, but specifically in relation to those of Factors A and B. Do they make sense as an overall set? Can we identify gaps in logic, scale, information, and so on? Do we need to bring in other factors and outcomes in order to complete our understanding? As outlined, the rigid process structure we set out here should not become a straightjacket. It is designed to enable and support creative and lateral thinking, not exclude it. However, whatever confirmation, augmentation, amendment or addition to the Stage 4 extreme outcomes is developed here, the recording should again be methodical, on flip charts or large sheets of paper for future reference as necessary.

On longer scenario projects that are not severely time-constrained – particularly where they involve multiple iterations of scenario generation with research undertaken between – this stage is expanded by consideration of a much wider set of extreme outcomes, derived from consideration of individual driving forces rather than just the clusters. We outline this variation in Chapter 4. In longer projects, this stage of scenario thinking can lead to much more focused analytic thinking and can provide "reality checks" on cause/effect relationships. In short projects with limited time and prior research, it can become an exercise in "holding a finger to the wind" for a more basic "sanity check".

Having reflected upon and refined the various sets of extreme outcomes in terms of general logic, we now move to build them into four internally-consistent, separate, but related scenario outlines.

## Stage 7: Scoping the scenarios

Drawing first upon the extreme outcomes of Factors A and B, we consider how the sets of conditions defined by the two extreme outcomes of each interact with each other in the four possible combinations (A1/B1, A1/B2, A2/B1 and A2/B2), in order to produce what – in simplistic terms – might be described as best/best, best/worst, worst/best and worst/worst "worlds" in which the future will unfold. Again, we brainstorm a very broad range of descriptors of each of these future "worlds". For each, we consider what would be the state of society, the economy, technology, national politics, local government, local business, employment, climate, migration, education, crime, transport, cost of living, optimism, pessimism, and such.

Arriving at these sets of descriptors involves critical discussion and debate, engaging with questions as to who, what, why, where and when, in order to build a logical structure to each future that can be shown to have some justifiable foundation for its possibility and plausibility in terms of what is currently either known or knowable. Adoption of a "devil's advocate" approach is highly valuable at this stage, and the group skeptic should be allowed free reign to probe and challenge – but *without* breaking the *ground rules* set out previously (p. 24).

At this stage, the group should draw upon all of the extreme outcomes for all the factors in order to give "body" to the emerging scenarios. This, again, involves critical discussion and debate on relationships of cause and effect, action and outcome, and chronology, since the aim is to place every significant outcome into the scenario (or scenarios) where it logically sits. Here, it should be clear that there are relationships between factors that will make some linkages immediately credible and others nonsensical. Also, there may be factors that were identified earlier as having a great impact, but as being highly predictable in terms of what that impact will be. Such factors will need to be incorporated into every scenario, with the actual impact fine-tuned as necessary in order to take account to any mediating impact from other factors.

---

**Example 2.8**

If we have a set of extreme outcomes that outline a world in which economic uncertainty and instability have led to governments adopting policies of protectionism through the application of non-tariff barriers, it would be unrealistic to match these to another set of extreme outcomes that describe a world of free trade that is blossoming due to the removal of tariff barriers.

---

Whilst not all linkages will be so obvious, the strategic conversation around the full range of issues will generally point to them fitting into one or two scenarios. Any item that falls into more than one scenario can be duplicated, if it is an important issue, or it can be placed where it has maximum impact.

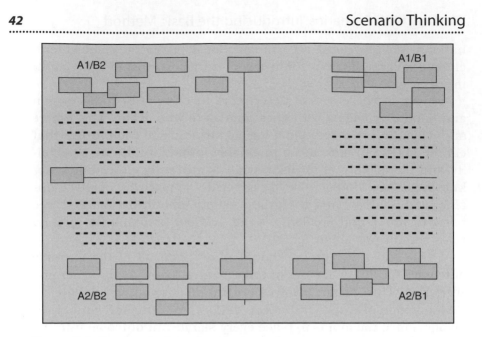

**Figure 2.6** Framing and scoping the scenarios

These combination descriptors form the basis of our four scenario storylines. At this stage, we would point out that the four scenarios that will be developed are *not* stand-alone stories or individual "predictions" of a possible future. Rather, they must be read as a group, framing the "limits of possibility" for what might reasonably be expected to happen over time. Together, they act as a set of tools for making sense of complexity and ambiguity, and for understanding the linkages across different areas of interest. Since history has never so far unfolded with a combination of all factors being at their best or worst, it is often in the mediation of some "good" outcomes by the impact of other "bad" ones (the A1/B2 and A2/B1 scenarios) that broader and more challenging possibilities for the future start to unfold.

## Stage 8: Developing the scenarios

At this stage, the scenario outlines consist of a set of descriptors of four possible futures framed by the interaction of Factors A and B, defined in terms of their extreme outcomes at the scenario horizon date. Now, we move to building the storylines that will show, logically and consistently, how we might get from where we are today to each of these future states. As the storylines are developed, some elements may be omitted from the stories where they add little or no impact, and detract from the core story. Remember, the focus of scenario analysis is on understanding the complexity and ambiguity of the world outside the organization. Many key decisions in organizations must address external factors that are not in the organization's grasp to impact to a great extent, if at all. However, decision-makers are often so focused on what is happening inside their own organizational worlds that they fail to grasp that what happens outside is more important in the long term.

In a full scenario project, the aim of the group is to outline a set of scenario stories that start in some coherent and plausible explanation of the present, then move through a series of further plausible and possible events in order to outline a set of futures that are internally consistent and coherent, and follow on from the logic of the events outlined. Remember, there are events in the future that – barring the unknowable (which scenarios do not deal with) – *will* happen, often with known key actors.

---

**Example 2.9**

We know at the time of writing that there *will* be presidential elections in the US in November 2012, November 2016 and every four years thereafter. At this time, we know that, barring the unknowable, Barack Obama *will* be his party's candidate in 2012, since he will be eligible to stand for re-election and, unlike the UK and Australia, there is no history of incumbent leaders being deposed by their own party. We also know that Barack Obama will *not* be a candidate in the 2016 election, since any President's tenure is limited to a maximum of two terms.

---

Whilst the dates of elections in other countries are not set in tablets of stone as in the US, there are often maximum terms between elections, so dates can be reasonably assumed in scenario development. Whilst we state here that scenarios do not deal with unknowable events, you may say that it is often these very occurrences that have the greatest impact on what follows. For example, the events of 9/11 had a global impact on air travel globally. We will address these possibilities in Chapters 7 and 8. In addition, there are also trends that we may see as likely to continue – for example, that information technology will continue to get faster and more powerful ... but will continue to fail to deliver the results that its designers claim for it! These, like known events, can be incorporated, where relevant, into all scenarios.

In working as a group to develop the scenario storylines, it can be very helpful to set up a whiteboard or some other appropriate surface and to draw a time line for the scenario period. The various events that are considered and discussed can then be set out and discussed in relation to links of cause-and-effect and chronology. This is particularly helpful in enabling discussion of the cross-linkages between factors and events that have previously been located in different cluster groupings. (See Figure 2.7, for an illustration of the use of a time line.)

The key aim in writing scenarios is to grab the attention of the intended audience in order to convey clear, concise and plausible stories about what types of futures might unfold as a direct outcome of decisions made in the present and over time in relation to the focal issue. The ways in which this can be done are many. Scenarios can be presented as fairly simple texts that recount what might happen in future. They can be delivered as mock newspaper or magazine articles that recount what has already happened at the scenario end date. Scenarios can be presented as live performances to the target audience, or can take the form of

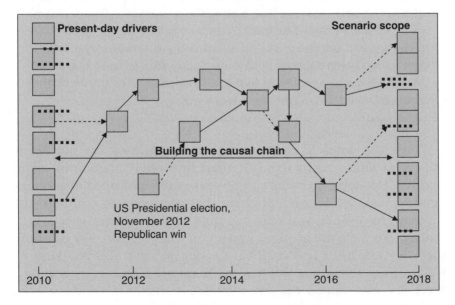

**Figure 2.7** Setting a scenario timeline

a telecast debate. Whatever approach is used, the focus is on the deep impact of the content, not the superficiality of the presentation media.

## BEYOND SCENARIO DEVELOPMENT: STRATEGIC DECISION-MAKING

Scenario stories in isolation serve no purpose *per se*. Whilst some approaches to scenario work place an emphasis on the scenario stories themselves as narratives of some "real world" futures, we see them, primarily, as providing a better understanding and a broader range of perspectives on the present. We view their function within the strategic planning process as threefold:

- to open up a wider set of perspectives on the present than currently exists;
- to provide a set of "wind tunnel" conditions under which to test existing strategies, in order to check their robustness under the different "climatic conditions" of the full range of plausible and possible futures that they outline; and
- to provide "feedback" from the future to the present in order to support the development of new strategies and plans in response to perceived alternative future business environments.

In each case, the aim is to support robust strategic planning that is not based upon a largely internally-focused analysis but, rather, that takes account of external drivers of the business environment. Scenarios are intended to enable decision-makers to identify opportunities and threats in the outside world more clearly. This enables them to consider the organization's strengths and to identify its weaknesses in relation to changing external conditions.

**Using the scenario report**, leaders can ask key personnel:

- What are the major business opportunities for the organization over the next *x* years?
- Are these consistent or variable across different future scenarios?

- What are the major external threats that stand in the way of achieving success?

Remember, what is an opportunity in one scenario may be a threat in another, so it is worth thinking of opportunities and threats in pairs.

Having identified the external opportunities and threats, consider:

- What are the organization's current strengths that will enable it to achieve success in all possible future scenarios?
- What are the weaknesses that will stand in the way of achieving success within any or all future scenarios?

Again, remember that what represents a strength in one particular future (e.g. being highly specialized in one area) may be a weakness in another (there is no demand for this!)

Contributions from individuals can be compiled into a report that is structured around key themes and issues, serving as an interactive document for future planning/strategy meetings.

# CHAPTER 3

# Incorporating Stakeholder Values and Facilitating Critique of Scenario Storylines

As we have seen, scenarios are conventionally constructed using three sources of input from the minds of the scenario team:

- views on the pre-determined elements of the future (such as the proportion of the population that will be in the age band 65 years+ over the next, say, 20 years);
- views on the critical uncertainties in the future – whose resolution, one way or the other, will have a large impact; and
- the actions of stakeholders, customers, regulators, competitors, and so on, as they react to unfolding events, in order to preserve and enhance their own interests.

These inputs are then combined in a recipe-like fashion to construct four scenarios.

## AVAILABILITY BIAS

One issue, though, is the extent to which the scenario team's views of these trends and uncertainties that will be present in the future are simply replications of current, media-emphasized concerns. For example, in early 2011, there are global concerns with the ongoing fall-out from the global financial crisis of 2008. Current concern in Europe is focused on the impact of the global financial crisis on the economies in Greece, Italy and Portugal. In the US, it is on the risk of a double-dip recession. In Australia, the main concern is whether the country can continue to avoid the worst impacts of the global financial crisis. In the second quarter of 2010, the grounding of most airplanes in Europe due to the eruption of an Icelandic volcano was to the fore in people's minds as an ongoing issue, but one that fluctuated in significance as the level of activity of the volcano and the scale of perceived threat in the aviation industry changed on a weekly, if not daily, basis. By the end of the third quarter of the year, this disruption was more or less confined to history. Less recent but still vivid high-impact events – such as the terrorist attacks on the Twin Towers in New York and the transport systems of London – continue to impact upon perceptions of what the future might hold.

Events of the type outlined will tend to be included, in some general form, in the development of scenarios by members of scenario teams dealing with a complex problem that is viewed in any way as being impacted by them. By contrast, non-vivid events are less likely to be replicated in constructed scenarios. For example, consider Figure 3.1, which shows the two factors that dominated one European bank's mortgage business scenarios that were developed in early 2008 – just months before the global financial crisis meltdown. Here, the top executives of the bank were concerned about the need to develop mortgage products that were multigenerational – such that succeeding generations would pay off the mortgage debt on a purchased residential property. The executives were also concerned that the food supermarkets, who already offered loans and bank accounts, would start to offer mortgages direct to their customers. No mention was made of the fragility of the housing market and its year-by-year increase in prices. Residential house prices were assumed to be on a steady, upward trajectory – just has they had been since 2001. The last downturn in the housing market had been from 1989 to 2001, when residential house prices lost 35% of their value. But this event was over seven years in the past, and so less vivid than the recent steady growth in house prices.

Towards the end of the first decade of the twenty-first century, European and US housing lenders' thinking was influenced by a very different range of factors, such as the collapse in demand for and value of many properties, levels of default in mortgage payments, and weakness of some European economies outlined above. At the same time, in Australia, there was officially no recession and the economy remained strong. Here, demand for housing in major cities like Melbourne outstripped supply, house prices remained on the up and up, inner city residencies sold for far above the asking price, and property values continued to rise at well above the rate of inflation. Only in the last weeks of the decade, as 2011

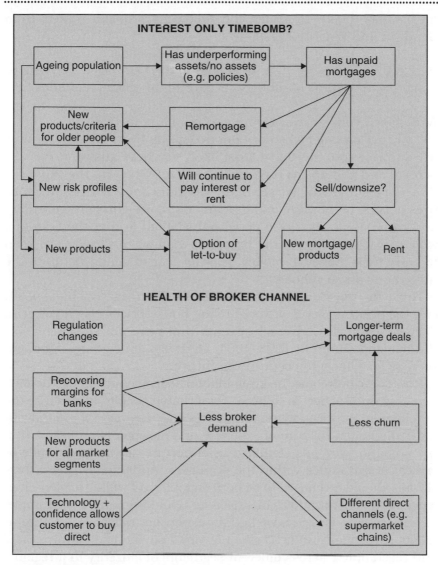

**Figure 3.1** Two high-impact, high-uncertainty clusters
Note: These two high-impact, high-uncertainty clusters dominated the European bank's mortgage business scenarios in early 2008, just before the global financial melt-down.
Source: Goodwin and Wright (2010).

approached, was there an indication that – whilst no collapse was foreseen – there might actually be limits to this runaway demand.

What is the cause of this replication, in the future, of elements of the present and recent past? The term for this effect is the "availability bias". Consider the following problem (taken from Goodwin and Wright, 2009):

> In 2007, what percentage of people in the USA (aged 12 years or over) were victims of robbery, according to official statistics?

Write down your answer before you read any further.

If you are a reader who does not live in the USA, then the answer will surprise you. It is 0.2%. Most likely you have answered over 10 percent and perhaps as high as 30 percent. What are the causes of this over-estimation? We see many US films and TV series in countries outside of the USA, and in many there are gunfights, murders and car chases. Thus, the perceived wisdom is that the USA is a violent place. In fact, many first-time visitors to Florida are keen to carry their money in money belts for fear of falling victim to the ubiquitous street robbery!

Thus, for the European bank and its mortgage business leaders, the previous seven years of rising house prices was a powerful decision context. Conversely, events that were not so salient, like the housing slump in 1998–2001, were less immediate – and, so, seen as less likely to occur in the future.

How do we overcome the availability bias in scenario construction? One way, in practice, is to have "remarkable people" involved in the development process. By remarkable people, we mean those individuals who hold a mixture of expertise and viewpoints on issues that the scenario team has identified as either pre-determined trends or critical uncertainties within the scenarios. Additionally, these individuals should be chosen to be both capable and willing to offer challenge to the organization's business-as-usual thinking. For example, in one scenario exercise, we had an expert on Information Communication Technologies (ICT) give his views on the likely future price and reach of ICT across different segments of citizenry in a region – segmented in terms of age, education, wealth and social class. This input stretched the thinking of the scenario team – who had no prior understanding of the immediacy and strength of technological innovation that would produce intuitive-to-use, cheap-to-purchase technology. But, even so, experts' predictions can be wrong, as the following quotations illustrate (Cerf and Navasky, 1998):

> *Heavier than air flying machines are impossible.*
> (Lord Kelvin, Mathematician/physicist, 1895)

*Everything that can be invented has been invented.*
(Charles H. Duell, Commissioner US Patent Office, 1899)

*Worldwide demand for cars will never exceed one million, primarily because of a limitation in the number of available chauffeurs.*
(Research prediction, Mercedes-Benz, 1900)

*A severe depression like that of 1920–21 is outside the range of probability.*
(Harvard Economic Society, 1929)

*Very interesting, Whittle, my boy, but it will never work.*
(Professor of Aeronautical Engineering, Cambridge to Sir Frank Whittle, inventor of the turbojet engine, 1930)

*I think there is a world market for about 5 computers.*
(Thomas Watson, Chairman, IBM, 1943)

There is no reason for any individual to have a computer in their home.
(Ken Olson, President, Digital Equipment, 1977)

*The world market for computers is about 275,000.*
(John Ackers, Chairman, IBM, 1983)

These quotations illustrate that even experts can be trapped by their own expertise and can become unable to perceive the possibility of radical change in the industries that they know so well. This problem has been labeled as a "framing bias".

## FRAMING BIAS

"Framing" is the equivalent of seeing a visual scene through a particular window frame. Imagine looking out onto a garden from the different windows of a house. Particular windows will reveal a different view of the garden. From some viewpoints, you will not see a person walk up the garden path; from other viewpoints you will. A particular, well-used frame will thus give a single perspective on a visual scene that, in fact, can be viewed from multiple perspectives. It follows that so-called "re-framing" will, perhaps, be beneficial and provide fresh insights to enhance the usual viewpoint. Challenge to familiar frames should thus be encouraged. One way to do this in a scenario development team is to have a heterogeneous set of team members. Another way is to structure the evaluation of individual viewpoints by facilitating critique or dissent. We will next illustrate both of these approaches to re-framing.

Consider the following two problems (taken from Tversky and Kahneman, 1981) and make a selection of what you consider to be the most appropriate and effective program to address each.

---

### Decision problem 1

Imagine that the US is preparing for the outbreak of an unusual viral disease that is expected to kill 600 people. Two alternative programs to combat the disease have been proposed. Assume that the exact scientific estimate of the consequences of the programs is as follows:

- If Program A is adopted, 200 will be saved;
- If Program B is adopted, there is 1/3 probability that 600 people will be saved, and a 2/3 probability that no people will be saved.

Which program would you select?

### Decision problem 2

Imagine that the US is preparing for the outbreak of an unusual viral disease that is expected to kill 600 people. Two alternative programs to combat the disease have been proposed. Assume that the exact scientific estimate of the consequences of the programs is as follows:

- If Program C is adopted, 400 people will die;
- If Program D is adopted, there is a 1/3 probability that nobody will die, and a 2/3 probability that 600 people will die.

Which program would you select?

---

Most people, when shown Decision problem 1, choose Program A; by contrast, most people, when shown Decision problem 2, choose Program D.

Now, look carefully at the two decision problems. You will see that, in fact, they are different versions of a single problem – like different frames on an identical scene. The only difference between the two is that Problem 1 emphazises lives saved whilst Problem 2 emphasizes lives lost. Close consideration of the numbers shows that Option A is identical to Option C, and also that Option B is identical to Option D. Changes in a purely verbal emphasis – "lives saved" changed to "lives lost" – lead the decision-maker to make very different decisions. Note that neither the first nor second options can be shown to be the best option, only that options A and C are formally identical, as are Options B and D. In other words, subtle differences in the framing of a decision problem can change the subsequent preferred decision selected by an individual. Changes in verbal emphases can enable politicians, pressure groups and politically motivated media to mold public opinion. For example, an overrun of US$1.9 billion on a US$50 billion defense project could be presented in two ways:

- The defense project stayed within 5% of budget – a frame of on-target defense spending;
- The defense project over-ran the budget by US$1.9 billion – a frame of a clear over-run in defense spending.

## The benefits of heterogeneity in opinions

Ilan Yaniv (2011) conducted a study in a group setting that varied the framings of those reading about a formally-identical decision, similar to the one about the US preparing for the outbreak of a viral disease given in Decision problems 1 and 2. Yaniv labeled as homogeneous those groups of individuals who were set up to view the decision in just one way. By contrast, the heterogeneous groups were made up of individuals who were set up to have a mix of alternative frames on the formally-identical decision. In his study, Yaniv demonstrated that subsequent discussion – focused on identifying the best decision – within the two types of groups led to:

- an intensification of a single-frame viewpoint in the homogeneous group; and
- the facilitation of multiple-frame viewpoints within most of the individual group members in the heterogeneous groupings.

The implications of Yaniv's findings are, we think, fundamental for the design of an effective scenario construction process. Invalid consensus in same-thinking scenario teams will increase the team's confidence in the constructed futures, but this confidence could be misplaced. The practical implications of this conclusion are that:

1.   Those in the scenario team should be chosen to represent different viewpoints. For example, participants could be invited from all divisions of an organization. In this way, the likelihood that multiple frames on a situation will be generated within individual members of the scenario team is increased.

2.   The facilitation process underlying scenario construction should act to both preserve and enhance any differences in team members' viewpoints. As far as possible, the participants should be of equal status – or, at least, feel able to express minority viewpoints without fear. In this way, the action of group processes that normally act to generate agreement – to preserve friendly relations among group members – will be dampened.

3.   Remarkable people should be brought into the process wherever possible, in order to prompt and promote challenge to business-as-usual thinking.

4.   The scenario development process should set "rules of engagement" for participants, such that all participants, no matter how senior, are allowed broadly equal air-time to present their input. One way that this can be achieved is using the "round robin" approach in the first stages of the scenario production, where uncertainties and trends are identified. As we have seen in Chapters 1 and 2, the role of the facilitator is a crucial one in allowing less-senior and quiet individuals air-time relative to dominant and talkative participants. Throughout the process, questions of clarification should be allowed, but challenges that others are "talking nonsense" should be proscribed.

In this way, the key resource of the scenario team – the thoughts and creativity of the group members – will be preserved, shared, and enhanced.


## ENHANCING STAKEHOLDER ANALYSIS USING ROLE-PLAYING

Can more be done to create heterogeneity of viewpoints? One additional way is to ask participants to consider, in detail, the interests of the stakeholders that have been identified earlier in the scenario development process.

One certainty is that human motivation and self-interest will be a key causal factor in determining the characteristics of the future. Maslow's "theory of human motivation" (Maslow, 1943) was a goal-based conceptualization. Maslow argued that the basic needs of humans are physiologically-based – the need for food, water, sleep and sex. If the physiological needs are relatively well-satiated, then physical safety needs become the focus of attention. If both physiological and safety needs are relatively well-satisfied, then the need for love, affection and belongingness become a focus. The next set of needs in Maslow's hierarchy is the need for esteem from others. The ultimate need is that of self-actualization – the desire for self-fulfillment and the desire to know and understand. Maslow's theory was put forward as a general theory of human motivation – one that transcends nationalities and cultures.

From this short summary of Maslow's theory, we can develop a basis for anticipating the nature of the future: individuals and organizations will strive to satisfy the hierarchy of needs. Thus, the development of constant water supplies aids the satisfaction of physiological and safety needs. The invention and development of mass immunization aids the satisfaction of safety needs. The invention and development of the Internet aids the satisfaction of the need for self-actualization – for example, instant access to knowledge. The development of airline services allows, for example, contact with family and business colleagues – thus, in part, satisfying the needs for love, affection and belongingness.

Specific technological developments cannot be predicted, but general technological development can, since any development will be to satisfy human needs. For example, suppose that the effect of an unknown event is the end of international air travel. How would self-interested humans react? Managers still need to hold face-to-face meetings with overseas colleagues, and we could also expect enterprising people to respond to this new situation. The result would likely be a huge growth in the use of video conferencing, and the associated enhancement of the availability and quality of such services. In short, basic human motivations should be modeled and analyzed in an enhanced scenario planning methodology. Understanding human motivations can provide a primary insight into the nature of an unfolding future.

Green and Armstrong (2011) studied the worth of inviting individuals to "stand in the other person's shoes" (p. 75). Did this instruction give those individuals useful insights into the quality of their initial intuitive judgments? Green and Armstrong's focus was on "forecasting" the actual decisions made in real, but historic, conflict situations, with participants instructed to indicate "which decision you think that each party in the situation would prefer to be made and how likely is it that each party's decision will actually occur". An example conflict situation was that of angry nurses increasing their pay demand and threatening further strike action after specialist nurses and junior doctors received a large pay increase. Participants in the role-thinking were asked to predict the outcome of negotiations between the stakeholder groupings after having read role descriptions of each grouping. The role descriptions detailed recent context and actions. However, the directive to participants to engage in "role-thinking" resulted in forecasts that were no more accurate than guesses. In contrast, when students were required to become more engaged with the conflict situations – by "role-playing" or simulating the interactions between participants in the conflicts – the predictive accuracy of the role players' in-role decisions reached 90 percent. In the role-playing simulation, each student was assigned a single role, and the role-players interacted with each other in a similar way to actors on a stage.

Somehow, role-playing brought out the best from the university students – in that their simulations of conflict situations resulted in resolutions of the conflicts that were close to real-life resolutions. Green and Armstrong's students could not be expected to have strong technical or domain knowledge about each, or all, of the conflict situations. Intuitively, an understanding/enactment of stakeholder motivations/behavior seems more fundamental to predicting/resolving the actual outcomes of conflicts than either technical or domain knowledge. Intuitively, it would seem that one's own experiences of the past resolution of conflicts – perhaps as recalled or previously experienced, and including personal as well as non-personal conflicts – would be a strong guide to the prediction/resolution of the outcomes of conflicts, since Maslow's hierarchy of needs underpins all of human behavior. Thus, it seems intuitively reasonable that only when individuals are enmeshed in role-play simulations will the relevance of this experience become obvious – since Green and Armstrong's conflicts will, initially, have been seen as outside the domain of this experience at a superficial, face-content level.

All these studies, therefore, speak in one way or another to the benefits of heterogeneity in groups to aid scenario development, and of the value of using role-playing to create artificial heterogeneity when this does not exist.

As we have discussed, scenario method explores the complex relationship between social, economic, technological, environmental and political factors from multiple perspectives; enables sense-making of their interactions; and provides a vehicle for the development of plausible futures that may impact on the focal organization. The conventional scenario approach entails some consideration of stakeholder values and actions to add realism to already-constructed scenarios but, in practice, this may be limited to those stakeholders that are directly involved in the exercise. For example, van der Heijden *et al.* (2002: 219) state that stakeholder analysis is an optional addition to the "mix" of ingredients; as "a tool to be used in parallel with the scenario process, as and when members of the scenario team find it useful". Stakeholders, according to the "narrow" (Freeman, 1994) definition, include the focal organization's competitors, customers, regulators, and so on – that is, those with direct financial, executive or regulatory interests in an unfolding scenario.

Wright and Goodwin (2009) have argued for a more intense focus on stakeholder analysis within the scenario development process, as the likely actions of stakeholders to enhance and preserve their own interests in a particular unfolding scenario are thought through. These authors emphasize the need to consider Maslow's hierarchy of needs in order to understand the likely reactions of particular stakeholder groupings to the unfolding sequence of events within a particular scenario storyline.

However, the scenario team's consideration of stakeholders who are not central to the scenario storyline may be limited, or non-existent. A broad view, however, leads to consideration of those stakeholders that lack direct links to the organization, but who can either affect of be affected by its strategies, policies, programs and activities, whether now or in the future. For example, Cairns *et al.* (2010) advocate the interrogation of the scenario stories from the perspective of the full range of involved and affected actors. They achieve this through application of the "value-rational" question framework for phonetic inquiry developed by Danish academic, Bent Flyvbjerg (2001, 2003). This framework focuses on the interests of society at large in relation to the future towards which a particular unfolding scenario leads:

- whether or not the scenario's outcomes are desirable;
- what if anything we should do about the outcomes; and, most pertinently,
- who gains and who loses from unfolding events.

Winners achieve their outcomes by exercise of power to maintain or enhance their interests. For example, one multi-national enterprise oversees the assembly of televisions from world-sourced flat panel displays and electrical components. By establishing the most efficient and effective value chains, cheaply-priced new technology is brought to western consumers. However, there are other, less-salient, stakeholders, including:

- villagers who melt the plastic coating off the copper wires within the now-redundant cathode-ray tube televisions/monitors to get at the valuable copper; and
- governments who may, or may not, put in place regulations to prevent damage to health from the four-to-six pounds weight of lead in every broken cathode ray tube from televisions or monitors.

Cairns *et al.* (2010) advocate structuring analysis of developed scenarios using a matrix that lists the first-cut scenarios along the top row of a matrix (each summarized under Flyvbjerg's question, "*Where are we going?*"). The full range of stakeholders is then inserted down the left-hand column. Within each box that marks an intersection of a scenario and a stakeholder group, we consider two issues:

- the impact of the unfolding future on the actor group's interests and values: "*Is this development desirable?*"
- the likely action/reaction of the group to the particular unfolding future: "*What, if anything, should we do about it?*", where "we" is the particular stakeholder group.

Use of role-playing, rather than role-thinking, enables the scenario team to become more sensitized to the plight of each of the groups of stakeholders, and to become aware of the degree of power of action that each of them has to preserve or enhance their own interests as a particular scenario unfolds. On this basis, at the foot of the matrix, they consider responses to the final question: *"Who gains and who loses, and by which mechanisms of power?"* The following step-by-step method places stakeholder analysis at the core of the scenario development process:

- Stage 1: Construct provisional scenarios out of the critical uncertainties and pre-determined elements; identify the stake-holders;
- Stage 2: Assign each stakeholder role to an individual who comes from outside the original scenario team;
- Stage 3: Ask each stakeholder to state how they would react, in role, to an unfolding event in a the scenario storyline;
- Stage 4: Share this information with other stakeholders and add it to the enhanced scenario storyline; then share these enhanced storylines with all stakeholders;
- Stage 5: Repeat Stages 3 and 4 until the participants are exhausted with the task.

In Chapters 4 and 5, we extend and develop stakeholder analysis using Flyvbjerg's perspective, and show how this enhancement can allow the scenario team to become more aware of both:

- the consequences to (and likely reactions of) various stake-holder groupings to particular unfolding scenarios; and
- the consequences to (and likely reactions of) various stakeholder groupings to the self-interested actions of the focal organization.

Apart from role-playing, what other methods can a scenario team use to create debate and challenge? In the next section, we broaden our discussion of role-playing to evaluate other group-based methodologies to enhance judgment and decision-making. We draw out implications for improving scenario thinking.

## GROUP DECISION-MAKING RESEARCH AND SCENARIO DEVELOPMENT

Role-playing can provide valuable insights into the likely thoughts and actions of stakeholder grouping as the events in a particular scenario unfold. As such, stakeholder analysis challenges and enhances the first generation scenarios, which are based solely on the interaction of uncertainties (as they resolve themselves one way or another) and pre-determined elements over time. But challenge to the scenario storylines can be made more focused, and it is to methods that can help achieve this focus that we now turn.

Schweiger *et al.* (1986) discuss two methods that systematically introduce *conflict* and *debate* in a management team by using two sub-groups that role-play. In *dialectical inquiry*, the sub-groups develop alternative strategies or decisions, and then later come together to debate the assumptions and recommendations of the alternative positions on an issue. In *devil's advocacy*, one sub-group offers a proposal for a strategy or decision. Next, the other sub-group plays devil's advocate, critically probing all elements and recommendations in the first sub-group's proposal. Both methods encourage the group members to:

- generate alternative courses of action; and
- minimize any group-based tendency towards early agreement on an option.

Without such structured critique, in order to preserve harmonious relations in the group, members tend not to voice critical thoughts. Research has shown that use of both methods will develop a high-level of understanding of the final group decision amongst group members.

However, there are potential problems with the role-playing of challenge and dissent within a group. Challenges need to be firmly focused on factual information because the personalities of individual group members can, inappropriately, become the focus of discussion. For example, some group members might be labeled as argumentative or dogmatic, thus leading to an emotional backlash from the named individual.

Schweiger *et al.* (1989) compared dialectical inquiry and devil's advocacy to a non-adversarial approach to decision making, where decisions were simply discussed with the aim of achieving a consensus amongst group members. Questionnaire ratings by group participants revealed that the two conflict-based approaches were rated higher in terms of producing better recommendations and better questioning of assumptions. Formalizing and legitimizing conflict by use of role-playing improves perceptions of the quality of the final outcome of group decision-making. However, whilst conflict can improve perceived decision quality, it may weaken the ability of the group to work together in the future, if the role-playing is not sensitively managed. Also, as Nemeth *et al.* (2001) document, authentic – rather than role-played – minority dissent, when correctly managed, is superior to role-playing interventions in stimulating a greater search for information on all sides of an issue by members of the group. But, generally, the authentic dissenter has been found to be disliked, even when she/he has been shown to stimulate better thought processes. Since the implementation of decisions rests on securing the subsequent cooperation of involved parties, the facilitator must make it clear to group participants that the role-playing exercise was just that – role-playing, and that group members *may not*, in fact, hold the views that they verbalized during the exercise.

We turn now to discuss the implications of these findings on group decision-making for scenario development. In practice, scenario development sometimes involves a scenario team composed of representatives from multiple agencies – that is, the scenario team is initially formed from a heterogeneous constituency. Cairns *et al.* (2006) developed scenarios for the use of ICT by citizens in their future interaction with local government. The scenario team incorporated representatives from an organization who had views on the attitudes/preferences of senior citizens, representatives from small and large businesses who were geographically located in the local government area, representatives from information communication technology companies, and so on. At the time, we argued that the process of scenario planning can provide a non-adversarial common viewpoint to unite what may, initially, be fragmented groupings. Now, in terms of our current analysis, we would argue that the fragmentation should, instead, be conserved – at least, until the point when any action response to the constructed set of scenarios is debated (see Goodwin and Wright, 2010). In that way, also, debate and challenge will be enhanced and, as we have discussed, debate and challenge are the key to the critical evaluation of assumptions.

In the more usual scenario development activity, conducted within a single organization, the conventional process results in the initial development of four skeleton scenarios that are then each fleshed-out by one of four sub-groups. However, since differences in worldviews between these sub-groups are likely to be small, we recommend that, once a particular scenario is fully-developed, it should then be given an adversarial critique by one or more of the other sub-groups. In this way, also, the systematic introduction of conflict and challenge is likely to enhance the quality of the finally-developed scenarios.

The following, step-by-step, method can introduce useful conflict and dissent into the scenario development process.

- Stage 1: Construct provisional scenarios out of the critical uncertainties and pre-determined elements;
- Stage 2: Divide the scenario team into four sub-groups and ask each to develop one of the four skeleton scenarios in detail. Members of the sub-groups should have, if possible, quite different perspectives on the issue of concern that was the basis for the overall scenario exercise. We recommend that each sub-group should be differentiated from the others in terms of the spread of heterogeneity – although, in practice, the allocation of individuals to groups must be a pragmatic process;
- Stage 3: Develop the scenario storylines using the enhanced stakeholder analysis method detailed earlier (p. 54);
- Stage 4: Ask each of the four sub-groups to present their developed scenario to all sub-groups in a plenary session;
- Stage 5: Ask each of the four sub-groups to prepare either:
  - a critique of each of the three other scenarios, or
  - alternative developments within the storylines of each of the three other scenarios;
- Stage 6: Reconvene the scenario team to hear the critiques or alternative developments;
- Stage 7: Ask each of the four original sub-groups to reconsider and revise the scenario storylines developed at Stage 3;
- As an optional eighth stage, it may be possible to engage non-participant representatives from the affected stakeholder groupings (that have been identified earlier in the scenario development process) to read and also provide critiques of the storylines.

## SUMMARY

This chapter has considered the degree to which availability bias and framing bias in the scenario team's thinking will result in scenarios that replicate, in the future, the concerns of the present. We concluded that there are great benefits in securing heterogeneity of opinions within the scenario team. Heterogeneity can be enhanced by including inputs by remarkable people to challenge the views of the scenario team on the nature of the identified uncertainties and pre-determined elements of the scenarios. Heterogeneity can be preserved by ensuring that all participants have equal air-time in the scenario development process. Artificial heterogeneity can be introduced by requiring individual scenario team members to role-play stakeholders, as a stakeholder reacts to unfolding events in order to protect or enhance their own interests and needs. All this will provide the scenario team with multiple framings on emerging situations within particular scenarios. Finally, use of dialectical inquiry and devil's advocacy methods will allow the developing scenario storylines to be critically evaluated and challenged. In these ways, the overall quality of the scenarios will be enhanced; the final scenarios will be more detailed, and the causal relationships in the scenario storylines will be made more realistic and compelling.

# Understanding Stakeholder Viewpoints

In the previous chapter, we showed that perceptions of a problem issue are frequently colored and constrained by images of recent high-profile events, and are influenced and molded by the different ways in which the same information can be presented. We illustrated how even "expert" views on a subject can subsequently be proven dramatically wrong. We also outlined the benefits of expanding thinking in scenario projects, moving beyond the "bounded rationality" of directly-involved stakeholders; executives, senior managers and experts in the particular problem field; and bringing in a wider range of affected and interested stakeholders. Having introduced some thoughts on how these issues can be made explicit and addressed, we develop these ideas in this chapter. First, we discuss not only various ways in which the same issue might be understood differently by different groups and individuals, but also how these differences might have a fundamental impact on just how uncertain – or how certain – its outcomes might be considered to be. Second, we consider in greater detail the issue of language and its use. Here, we look at how the same words and phrases can mean very different things to different people, even when they think they all speak the same language. Finally, we present a range of strategies for mitigating the risks inherent in such multiple interpretations and potential misunderstandings.

## DEVELOPING SHARED UNDERSTANDING OF WHAT IS NOT KNOWN AND UNDERSTOOD

Whilst the "expert" predictions we presented in Chapter 3 might seem quite amusing in hindsight, they represent a fatal flaw in human understanding that can have severe consequences on how a problem is addressed. Walker *et al.* (2010) have developed a taxonomy of "levels of uncertainty", ranging from Level 1 to Level 4, which is useful in explaining the value of scenarios:

- *Level 1* uncertainties are defined as relatively minor – as representing "a clear enough future" set within a "single system model" whereby outcomes can be estimated with reasonable accuracy;
- *Level 2* uncertainties display "alternative futures" but, again, within a single system in which probability estimates can be applied with confidence.

*Levels 3 and 4* uncertainties are described as representing "deep uncertainty".

- *Level 3* uncertainties are described as "a multiplicity of plausible futures", in which multiple systems interact, but in which we can identify "a known range of outcomes". Scenario thinking enables us not only to determine this range of outcomes, but also to understand the different causal networks that will lead towards each;
- *Level 4* uncertainties lead us to an "unknown future" in which we don't understand the system: we know only that there is something, or are some things, that we know we don't know. Other than engaging with the completely unknowable, scenario method also helps us to start to identify what it is that we don't know, and to convert Level 4 uncertainties into comprehensible Level 3 issues.

In this book, we set out scenario method as an approach to dealing with Level 3 and Level 4 "deep uncertainties", in order to test existing strategies and to inform development of flexible new strategies and adaptive plans for facing up to these uncertainties. However, history shows that what are, in fact, Levels 3 and 4 business problems are not always recognized as such, and they are frequently presented in terms that indicated much greater certainty about their outcomes.

---

**Example 4.1**

As outlined in Chapter 3, the CEOs of major computer manufacturers have, at different times, seen the future market for their companies' core product as capable of being defined with accuracy at either 5 or

275,000 units. These CEOs envisioned a Level 1 uncertainty. Here, there was "a clear enough future" where the outcome was defined by a "point estimate". There may have been some defined confidence interval. That is to say, any variation from the 5 or 275,000 was defined in terms of probability, set within fairly narrow boundaries of error. However, neither of these predictions for the global market in computers allowed space for thinking on what has actually happened: where a single household may have 5 or more computers and 275,000 computers would barely meet the demand of a small town.

How can we avoid such misplaced confidence?

Before launching into any analytic project to explore a key focal issue of concern, the project sponsor must first define the issue with clarity. They should set it out in terms of:

- the central process, product or plan that forms the crux of the issue; and
- the nature and extent of the uncertainty that is considered to exist in relation to its future.

The individual should think carefully about whether this uncertainty can be defined in terms of a Level 1 prediction, with parameters for variation around this. Or, can it be resolved as group of Level 2 possibilities with probability estimates for each? However, she/he must be realistic in considering whether the issue can only be understood as a set of different Level 3 futures, each with a clear set of defined outcomes, or only by means of a Level 4 statement to the effect that we know only that there is something crucial that we don't yet know. In the contemporary business world, it may be seen as a weakness for senior managers to define a complex business problem in terms only of what is *not* known, rather than in terms of what *is* known – or is mistakenly thought to be known. You should remember that, as outlined in Chapter 3, individuals' perceptions of the degree of "certainty" or "uncertainty" about a particular issue are influenced by:

- how information is presented;
- the nature of group dynamics; and
- by degrees of homogeneity or heterogeneity within the group.

As such, there is often no clear or unanimous view of whether a particular uncertainty is set at a specific level. We suggest that an uncertainty should always be considered at the deepest proposed level, unless or until those that propose this level can be convinced by an evidence-based argument that it should be otherwise.

We would suggest that honest acknowledgement of gaps in knowledge is the only sensible risk management strategy, as illustrated by BP's failed decision-making in relation to the Deepwater Horizon disaster in the Gulf of Mexico – both before and after the blow-out. In Chapter 7, we offer guidance on how organizational decision-makers can seek to create "strategic defense" models to address potential high-impact strategic risks.

## THE "SOCIAL CONSTRUCTION OF UNCERTAINTY"

In Chapter 2, we introduced scenario method as a structured approach to exploring complex and ambiguous business problems in terms of the range of uncertainties that define them. We showed how to explore the "limits of possibility and plausibility" for them individually, and how to construct maps of causality and chronology in order to make them more easily understood and dealt with, without reduction or elimination of the constituent elements. Successful use of scenario method requires acceptance that it is not a sign of weakness to state that you don't know. Rather, it is an indication of a desire to know and understand more, openness to learn from others, and willingness to engage in group problem analysis and option appraisal.

Once the problem sponsor has a clear understanding of how she or he sees the uncertainty issue, it is possible to engage others in discussion and debate it. This discourse may show that the problem is a shared one, and that there is a common perception of the nature and limits of the uncertainty. Of course, it may be that the issue does not represent an uncertainty to everyone and that someone else has an answer to the problem. In this case, the next stage is to evaluate any proposed "right answer". This may lead to dissolution of the problem. It might also turn out that there is a shared recognition of a critical uncertainty existing, However, there may still be a diverse range of views on what the exact nature of the problem is, and on how best to address it. In this case, the stage of seeking a solution must be preceded by an exercise in seeking a shared understanding of the problem itself. Not only does opening up the issue to discussion in this way present the possibility that there is no single understanding of it; it may also be that group consideration of a complex and ambiguous problem may lead to a realization that it is even *more* complex and *more* ambiguous than first thought. Don't be concerned by this. Rather, be happy that you now know more about what you don't know.

In their seminal 1966 work on how organizations work as social systems, Peter Berger and Thomas Luckmann outlined the concept of the "social construction of reality". Their premise was that the reality of organizational life is not singular; that it is not objective and quantifiable as in the types of reality sought in the natural sciences. Rather, it is a wholly subjective entity, whereby what is considered to be "real" is derived from people's interactions and behaviors, and their developing beliefs and values. Reality, then, is both an outcome and a determinant of what happens in the organization through processes of reciprocity between members. In an ideal organizational world, the socially constructed reality will be common to members and will be understood in the same way by all. In this ideal situation, any problem and uncertainty will be understood in exactly the same way by each and every member, and the task of decision-making is one of finding the "right" answer – implying that all others are "wrong".

However, in an article in the journal *Human Relations*, Beech and Cairns (2001) reflect upon the nature of reality in a number of different organizations with which they engaged, and found that the notion of any "single reality" was problematic. They propose that, where members of an organization do espouse the concept of a single, shared reality of a complex problem, they most likely do so through exclusion or denial (not necessarily deliberate) of other possibilities. Their challenge to the notion of a single reality resonates with our challenge here: for you to think beyond what *is* known in relation to complex problems, and to consider the extent of what is *not* known. Their analysis of why such differences of understanding exist is relevant to how you engage with and under-stand others in a project situation.

Beech and Cairns outline and discuss three different ways in which "reality" can be divided. They term these theoretical inter-pretations as:

- multi-level realities;
- multiple realities; and
- "no-such-thing-as-reality".

Let us explain in basic, but relevant terms what these concepts mean in the context of a scenario project.

## COMMON ISSUE: SAME INTERPRETATION – DIFFERENT REASON

In the first conceptualization, an organizational situation is described in which there is a common major uncertainty to be faced, and there is a shared understanding that something – or, in this case, someone – is problematic to its resolution. However, it is only after more in-depth questioning – questioning that goes beyond what the problem is, to explore why it is thought to be a problem – that differences of viewpoint emerge.

---

**Example 4.2**

In this example, a local union representative is considered to be an "obstacle" to organizational change, both by local staff on site and by remote senior managers. To the latter group, he is seen to be "speaking for" a workforce that are resistant to change. However, to that workforce, he is seen as being a remnant of a previous culture that they have now outgrown, and as not speaking for them. In reality, his presence is an obstacle, not to change itself, but to effective communication between senior management and the workforce.

---

In this example, it is reasonable for management to assume that the union representative speaks for the workforce, and it may be thought careless of the workforce to maintain a non-representative union voice. The point of note for your work is that you should not assume that, because different groups express the same general views about the same issue, then they must have the same reasons for believing that it is important. For example, in one scenario project on the introduction of new information and communications technologies (ITCs), we found that various groups considered that this was "inevitable". For some, this inevitability was seen as a positive factor, to be embraced. For others, however, it was a cause for trepidation and fear of – yet another – technological failure to live up to expectations. The type of situation illustrated here will be recognized by many readers, but it is one that may be easily overlooked if there is no determination to surface such differences of opinion and interpretation at an early stage. It is essential to ensure that they are made explicit within the process of under-standing and defining the core business problem in the broadest possible terms.

## COMMON LANGUAGE: SAME WORDS – DIFFERENT MEANINGS

Moving beyond differences of reasoning that should be relatively straightforward to explore through more and clearer inter-group communication, let us now consider a more complex problem of language. In the next example, an organizational situation is outlined in which different groups of stakeholders appear to speak the same language – here, English. They use the same words to talk about core issues for the organization, but they attach very differ-ent meanings to them. These different meanings are considered to apply not only to a particular situation, as in the last example, but to arise from diverse professional cultures and sets of beliefs and values and, as such, to be likely to pervade all communication and interpretation by the particular group.

---

### Example 4.3

Here, two very different types of stakeholder have been brought together in a single organization through a process of merger and acquisition. A former state-owned utility company, staffed largely by long-serving engineers, has entered the emerging field of mobile telecommunications and Internet technologies through buying out new ventures, retaining the entrepreneurs who had set them up as members of the merged entity. Whilst both the engineer and entrepreneur groups use the same words, they each use them in very different ways. The engineers talk of "risk" as something dangerous, to be avoided at all costs through rigor and taking time. The entrepreneurs, on the other hand, talk of it as some-thing exciting, to be embraced with speed-to-market.

---

In this example, the engineering group's language was that of scientific rigor, seeking the "right" answer to problems, working under a safety regime with rigor and thoroughness in order to build cumulative knowledge within controlled parameters. To this group, risk was something to be minimized and designed out. On the other hand, the entrepreneurs spoke in terms of opportunities rather than answers. They encouraged innovation, speed-to-market, and short-term changes. To the engineers, the entrepreneurs appeared the epitome of risk! The article discusses how the different "languages" of the two groups not only caused issues between them, but led to very different – both negative – interpretations of a call for proactive business development from the new CEO. To the engineers, the call "Don't come to me for permission, come to me for forgiveness!" represented a license to the entrepreneurs to run riot with risky ventures. To the entrepreneurs, however, it appeared like a threat – don't venture too far outside the box or failure will be punished.

In drawing upon this example, we show that, even within the same organization, different stakeholders can read very different meanings into a few seemingly simple words. Worse, these meanings can be totally different from what the speaker intended. Here, the differences are not just of interpretation of words and behaviors, but of deeply embedded values and beliefs. This type of difference requires much greater attention and understanding, since it represents an ongoing and deeply engrained risk to successful organizational change.

In the context of a scenario project, the impact of problems of difference of meaning of "simple" words can emerge in several ways. First, if initial interviews are undertaken with different stakeholders then analyzed, as outlined in Chapter 2, and reported back anonymously, the meaning underpinning a statement may be taken very differently by the reader than was intended by the speaker.

---

**Example 4.4**

What is meant by: "We need to take steps to maximize the value of our offering"? Does this refer to shareholder value and stock price? Does it refer to customer value-for-money? Does it refer to utility value of a piece of equipment?

In the context of a group discussion, differences of meaning attached to the same words might operate in the same way, if statements like this go unquestioned: "What do you mean by 'value'?" However, they might also lead to situations of conflict, in which the different meanings are surfaced and expressed, but not in a constructive way. Our experience in scenario projects has, on more than one occasion, surfaced very different interpretations of the term "value", whether related to issues of finance, technology or human resources. It is essential that such differences are addressed and dealt with at an early stage in any scenario project. In the event of overt conflict in doing this, the facilitator must act decisively to defuse the situation by reference back to the ground rules of scenario projects.

## DIFFERENT PLACE OR AUDIENCE: CONFLICTING MESSAGES – SAME SPEAKER!

The final example is one in which one individual, or one group, presents very different interpretations of the same phenomenon when talking about it in different contexts or to different audiences. We must be clear that people here are not necessarily being considered as two-faced, lying or hypocritical. Rather, the aim is to show how individuals can appear perfectly relaxed with the concept of ambivalence – holding two different and seemingly contradictory ideas to be true and valued at the same time.

---

**Example 4.5**

Following the introduction of the "grey suit" as uniform in the hospital sector in the UK within a reorganization program, the business suit as uniform was spoken of by senior nursing staff as both a symbol of dedication to hands-on patient care and of detachment from it. In the first case, it is viewed as symbolizing their professionalism and authority. In the second, it represents a senior management that is aloof, detached and unconcerned with hands-on patient care.

---

Whilst to you, our reader, this may seem extraordinary, unbelievable and even morally unacceptable, we would urge you to consider your own lifestyle and your own beliefs and values. How many of us would not decry the social and economic deprivation of others in this world; would not argue against the use of "slave labor"? Yet, how many of us decline to purchase electronic goods or clothing that are dependent on such exploitation as a key part of their production?

## COPING WITH THE "MULTIPLE REALITIES" OF ORGANIZATIONAL LIFE

Beech and Cairns (2001) outline problematic issues where groups and individuals within a single organization hold to often very different socially-constructed realities. In concluding accounts of their various examples, they describe how, in some cases, the differences of understandings and interpretations can be overcome through active engagement in working together in order to address them. However, in other cases, management commitment to bringing about change was doomed to failure as individuals continued to "talk past each other", rather than to engage in meaningful exchange. As you set out to organize a scenario-based analysis of any complex and ambiguous organizational problem, it is incumbent upon you to watch out for the types of difference in language and meaning, and the underlying value system that these examples illustrate. Their unchecked existence could well spell failure for the project before it is even started.

Scenario method is designed to enable participants to address the language problems that have been outlined in a number of ways. First, any scenario project will involve the various stakeholders working together, openly discussing not only their knowledge and perceptions of key issues, but also their reasons for thinking as they do: "Why do you think that slave labor is immoral?" Second, they will be open to questions that seek clearer explanation of the meaning that is attached to terms: "What do you mean by 'slave labor'?" Third, the conversation should open up the possibility of ambivalent responses to issues, often through asking very simple questions: "Do you have a mobile phone?" Finally, if interviews have been conducted before the project and an interview report has been produced, the juxtaposition of different views on a particular issue should prompt debate on differences of knowledge and understanding, of opinion and interpretation, and of beliefs and values. It should also expose issues that are subject to ambivalent interpretation, albeit anonymously in this context.

As the initiator or facilitator of a scenario project, it goes without saying that the first place to look for possible problems of the type outlined is in the mirror! What is your own set of deeply-held beliefs and values; how do they influence the meaning that you attach to seemingly simple words and phrases?

## ACTIVELY SEEKING FURTHER REALITIES: BUILDING THE "BROAD" STAKEHOLDER APPROACH

In the last few sections, we have considered the problems of language in stakeholders' direct interaction with each other. However, the impacts of the fall-out from wicked problems that organizations face are not necessarily confined to directly-involved stakeholders. When disaster strikes – for example, as with the Deepwater Horizon drilling rig – it becomes apparent to the whole world that activities like oil exploration can impact a vast array of stakeholders, both human and non-human. It prompts those who are opposed to such operations to raise their voices, and it can also bring others to question and, seemingly, change their values and beliefs. However, without such disastrous failure, would there be a place in organizational planning for skeptical voices, let alone those who are opposed?

Contemporary business practice and management education engages with concepts of "corporate social responsibility", "triple bottom line" accounting, and "responsible management", probably more than at any time in the past. If matters are going to be addressed fully in relation to the broadest possible range of impacts of action, we suggest the need to adopt a "broad" stakeholder approach, as a minimum. Here, stakeholders are "(a)ny identifiable group or individual who can affect the achievement of an organization's objectives" (Freeman and Reed, 1983: 910). In addition, they are seen as "as individuals, human beings ... moral beings" (Freeman, 1994: 411), not as morally neutral and devoid of personal responsibility for organizational activities. What, then, is the impact of adopting a broad stakeholder view?

At the present time, there are major uncertainties facing humanity and its institutions that are subject to different interpretations and representations across stakeholder groups. Take, for example, the issue of climate change. For many in the scientific community, it is now taken as a certainty that climate change is happening and that it is primarily driven by human activity. Whilst they may be uncertain about the rate of change and the scale of its impacts, these scientists cannot easily understand why there is residual skepticism in society. Also, they cannot understand why the media gives voice to those that deny climate change. Others, however, point to past predictive failures of "experts", such as the Millennium Bug scare and failure to identify critical risks like the drug Thalidomide, and to selected events that appear to counter climate change – or, more specifically, "global warming" – claims, such as the harsh winters experienced across Europe and North America in 2010 and 2011.

If scenario method is to be truly inclusive and is to be used to explore the full range of possible and plausible futures, then the process must involve input from the broadest possible range of stakeholders. It must also incorporate consideration of every conceivable event and outcome that can impact the issue at hand over the selected time scale, so long as this outcome is considered possible and plausible. Of course, the question of possibility and plausibility will, in many cases, be highly contested. How, then, to address it?

There is no catch-all correct answer to this. Such areas of conflict must be addressed by applying the "ground rules" that we set out in Chapter 2. These are designed to promote and support open dialogue and debate between conflicting viewpoints, in an atmosphere of openness and acceptance of difference. Whilst they do not allow rejection of others' viewpoints as being "Rubbish!", they do allow for questions such as "Why do you think ...?", "How would ...?" and "Who might ...?". The group may reasonably choose to exclude any opinion that cannot in any way be supported in response to interrogation. However, any viewpoint that can in any way be justified to a reasonable extent must be included. Remember, the point of scenarios is to explore "the limits of possibility" without value judgment and without recourse to probability analysis.

## ADVANCED SCENARIO DEVELOPMENT: VALUE JUDGMENTS AND THE CRITICAL SCENARIO METHOD

As we stated at the outset, the incorporation of stakeholder analysis as a core element of scenario method is a key innovation in our approach. In other scenario approaches (cf. van der Heijden *et al.*, 2002), stakeholder analysis is an option, to be used as and when the scenario team think it appropriate. We would suggest that much organizational strategic analysis and decision-making is devoid of consideration of those stakeholders outside those immediately involved, and thereby exposes the organization to risk if and when the unexpected happens. Contemporary organizations must, more and more, be alert to and prepared for loss of reputation, bad PR and litigation that can arise from such happenings. Here, we advocate stakeholder analysis as an essential element of the process, if the scenario project is to serve as a vehicle for exploring "the limits of possibility" and be a tool for effective risk management.

Whilst we highlight that the scenario construction process is one of inclusiveness and accommodation of all perspectives, we acknowledge that the decision-making process that it is intended to inform will involve selection, exclusion and value-based judgments. Expanding upon ideas introduced in Chapter 3, we now consider in greater detail what Cairns *et al.* (2010) refer to as the "critical scenario method" (CSM) as an approach to interrogating scenarios from the perspectives of the full broad range of stakeholders. As we outlined in Chapter 3, Danish academic Bent Flyvbjerg (2001, 2003) has developed an approach to organizational inquiry that we draw upon in order to interrogate scenarios from the broad stakeholder perspective. This process of interrogation has its roots in the philosophy of Aristotle, in what he termed "phronēsis". This is an ancient Greek word that has no contemporary counterpart in Western languages, but which is generally translated as "prudence" or "practical wisdom". The principles of phronetic analysis are widely discussed across fields including medicine and education training, as well as in Flyvbjerg's social science contribution.

For Aristotle, prudence or practical wisdom should inform decisions made by key power-brokers based upon moral/ethical judgments about what is "good for man" (sic) – or for humanity. as we would now put it. As outlined, Flyvbjerg has developed a set of four seemingly simple questions that we can ask in relation to any project, strategy or intended set of actions in order to assess it in phronetic terms. These are:

- Where are we going?
- Is this development desirable?

- What, if anything, should we do about it?
- Who gains and who loses, and by which mechanisms of power?

(Flyvbjerg, 2003: 364)

As outlined in Chapter 3, the first of these questions can be addressed by scanning the end-state descriptions of the future world that any particular scenario outlines. However, the degree to which this exercise will address the broad stakeholder grouping will depend upon the extent to which the scenario analysis has covered the full range of PESTEL factors (see Chapter 2). If they have been explored in full, with regard for all stakeholders from the outset, there will be rich and "thick" descriptions of the future to which to refer. Where these rich descriptions cover not only key events and impacts of direct relevance to the narrow range of involved stakeholders, but also those that will be of significance to the broad stakeholder set, they will provide a strong basis for understanding the future from all stakeholder perspectives.

In addressing the second question, on the desirability or otherwise of a specific scenario, the stakeholder issue becomes more pertinent. What is desirable to, and to be strived for by one set of immediate stakeholders may result in effects that are highly *undesirable* for others who are more remote.

---

**Example 4.6**

It may be seen as highly desirable by stockholders for a mineral extraction company to put profit maximization at the centre of business planning. However, a drive for profit at the expense of other considerations may lead to a barren landscape in another country, the land stripped of its surface growth in order to access natural resources. This is likely to be highly undesirable for an indigenous people who see no benefit from the operations.

---

However, even closely related internal stakeholders may have very different views of what is or is not desirable. In the examples we have referred to in this chapter, from Beech and Cairns (2001), you can see illustrations of internal conflicts over desirability. Engagement in meaningful consideration of the breadth of stakeholder viewpoints on any issue is a challenge that should not be taken lightly. We have discussed some of the risks in Chapter 3 and have proposed some options for addressing them, such as role-playing and facilitating challenge by use of group-based processes.

The diversity, or otherwise, of the answers to the question of what is or is not desirable will determine the complexity of the third question of what, if anything, should be done about it. As outlined, if we adopt a truly phronetic approach, the answer to this question should be determined by consideration of what will offer the greater good to humanity.

We would highlight one very important point here. Whilst we set up scenario method as being value-free, addressing all possibilities equally, phronetic decision-making is not based upon a moral relativism, in which all values are given equal weighting. It involves making often difficult choices between competing alternatives, each offering some benefit to some stakeholders and, most likely, depriving others. The greater good sought from the process should be based upon long-term outcomes, not short-term results.

---

**Example 4.7**

The question of what, if anything, should be done about a particular problem can lead into a moral-ethical minefield. The practice of breaking up redundant ships by hand on the beaches of countries like Bangladesh and India has been widely criticized due to the presence of asbestos and other toxins in them (cf. Cairns, 2007; Cairns and Śliwa, 2008). Some call for a total ban on the practice. This seems sensible in health terms. But, the industry supplies most of the construction steel for Bangladesh, one of the world's poorest nations. What if that supply is cut? Also, it provides employment for workers from inland areas where there is no employment. What if they lose their jobs? How do they feed their families? We don't offer answers to these questions (neither do the authors referred to), but we do use them as examples of the possible knock-on effects of a "good" decision.

---

Having outlined the *theoretical* position in relation to the definition of "good" that underpins phronetic decision making, we acknowledge that human decision making, whether in organizations, politics or other groups, is rarely based upon consideration of what constitutes long-term good for all. This is where the fourth question comes into play: *Who gains and who loses, and by which mechanisms of power?*

In any complex problem situation, actual decision-making may be based upon short-term benefits, expediency, instrumentalism for personal gain, or any number of other factors. The key element of application of Flyvbjerg's question framework is that it lifts the veil of secrecy from such approaches. It prompts and supports decision-making that is grounded in broad social and environmental benefit analysis, and makes it transparent if other criteria take precedence.

The application of the fourth question – on winners, losers and power – will generate a different set of answers within each of the scenarios. For many projects, the answers within a business-as-usual context will be that the winners are shareholders or stock-holders, senior managers, major suppliers and the like. Losers might include workers in export processing zones in developing economies, communities who lose their land to resource exploitation, or workers who are retrenched or made redundant due to operational "efficiency" gains. The mechanisms of power might range from those of formal firm structures to country legislative frameworks and "structural adjustment" programs of the International Monetary Fund (IMF) and World Bank.

---

### Example 4.8

In the case of ship-breaking, let us consider one scenario. Say that, as a result of pressure by Greenpeace and other NGOs, there is a global ban on sending ships for breaking up on "third-world" beaches. Who might be winners? The NGOs would certainly declare themselves winners – and may consider the workers as "winners", having had their health protected through their actions. High-tech ship-breaking yards in "developed world" countries would presumably win – new, high value business. Who might be losers? These might be ship owners who have to pay for the breaking, rather than selling the ships for millions of dollars. They would be current yard owners, losing their source of revenue and profit. They might be workers, if they have no other source of livelihood and see feeding their families tomorrow as more important than their own long-term health. The governments of affected countries might be either winners or losers – winners if they can "blame" NGOs for an economically damaging but environmentally beneficial change, losers if they cannot provide longer-term alternative industry and employment. The mechanisms of power here are presumably those of NGOs working at a global level with intergovernmental agencies to push through internationally agreed and recognized legislative frameworks.

If the scenarios developed do, indeed, cover the full range of possibilities and are plausible, there should be at least one that is based upon, even if not fully meeting, the principles of phronetic inquiry. Here, the winners will be more widely distributed and the gains will be defined in less extreme terms than in a short-termist, stock-value maximization scenario. There will, of course, still be losers. Some of these will be "relative losers", such as the stock-holders who are still well-rewarded but who derive less financial gain than in alternative scenarios. Some may be absolute losers, being deprived of resources, opportunity or employment in order that the greater good will have been served. In this scenario, there will most likely be very different power plays than in others.

## SCENARIOS AS TOOLS FOR CONSOLIDATION OR FOR CHANGE

Based upon what we have outlined so far in this book, you can see that scenarios offer a strong tool for exploring the range of possible futures that might arise. As we have shown, the use of scenario method offers an escape from linear thinking on the future as an extension of the past, and from consideration of a single future based upon some form of probability analysis and predictive forecasting. At a basic level, scenario method enables organiza-tions to be better prepared for an uncertain future, and to assess the robustness of current strategies and plans across the range of possible and plausible futures. Thereafter, the introduction of stakeholder analysis into the scenario process enables organiza-tions to contemplate issues of who will make things happen; why they might do certain things, or not do other things; and, finally, who will be impacted and affected by different future events and outcomes.

At one extreme, effective application of scenario thinking can provide a vehicle for organizations to consolidate their current position in terms of market position, profitability, and so on. It can enable them to identify both opportunities and threats in the external environment under different prevailing future conditions, and to assess their current strengths and weaknesses within each set. The future-oriented business will then ensure that its strengths are reinforced and expanded as necessary in order to build resilience in the face of all identified threats.

Scenario method can also offer the opportunity to consider radical change for the future. Such change may be driven by an enlightened senior management or executive that sees that a business-as-usual model is not socially and ecologically sustainable, if the worst effects of continuing environmental degradation and resource depletion are to be avoided. However, in some scenarios it may be driven by interested external stakeholders with a vested interest in bringing about fundamental change to the way in which business operates. In some scenarios – extreme, but possible and plausible – these stakeholders may emerge as groups or individuals about whom the organization knows little or nothing at present, and cares even less.

As we have stated several times, scenario method offers one approach to risk analysis and appraisal that can be integrated into a comprehensive risk management framework for the organization.

## SUMMARY

In this chapter, we have outlined the notion of the "social construction" of reality, and how the "reality" of organizational life may be read and understood very differently by different groups and individuals within it. We then illustrated how seemingly simple matters of words and language can be sources of major problems in undertaking any project that involves multiple viewpoints and expressions. We showed that, even where people think they are talking the same language, whether English or Russian, it is possible that they will apply different meanings to the same words. Some of these different meanings may be based upon differences of disciplines, such as engineers or entrepreneurs, due to variations in the underpinning values and beliefs that each group holds to and that guide their decision-making. However, we also showed that individuals can adapt an ambivalent approach, where they hold seemingly contradictory things to be true at the same time. We highlighted the need for early recognition of the possibility of "multiple realities", and for addressing them through frank and open debate and discussion.

We then developed our presentation of the application of stakeholder analysis in scenario method, arguing for our approach of embedding engagement with the "broad" range of stakeholders as part of the process. Beyond the basic consideration of all stakeholders' interests in developing value-free scenarios, we turned to the option of a CSM that is used to inform a decision-making process that is grounded in consideration of values. Here, we outlined the theoretical concept of phronetic inquiry, which is directed towards morally- and ethically-grounded decision-making that seeks to steer the future towards one that is for the good of humanity in general, rather than a few stakeholders in particular.

We noted that scenarios can constitute either a tool in support of a program of consolidation, or a prompt for action towards radical change. In either case, if the approach outlined here is adopted in full, it will be apparent who the winners and losers will be from any course of action, and the nature of the power structures that drive the future.

In Chapter 5, we set out step-by-step procedures for undertaking more complex scenario projects, both broadening the scope of engagement with stakeholders, and delving deeper into understanding values and beliefs that underpin decisions and actions.

# Augmented Scenario Approaches: Delving Deeper and Stretching Wider

In this chapter, we set out the various stages and options for undertaking two augmented and more highly-developed scenario approaches. These are not stand-alone approaches, in that they each relate to and build upon the basic method outlined in Chapter 2. As such, they must be read in conjunction with Chapter 2 for implementation purposes, and only after Chapter 2 in terms of developing your overall understanding of scenario method. Additionally, the two approaches outlined do not stand apart from each other. They can each be implemented separately as extensions of the basic method, or they can be combined with each other and the basic method in order to bring both greater depth of understanding of the content that informs the analytic process, and greater breadth to consideration of the impacts of driving forces and events across human society and the natural environment over time. The second augmentation, which brings in consideration of "broad" stakeholder analysis (Freeman and Reed, 1983), demonstrates application of the "critical scenario method" (CSM) approach that we introduced in Chapter 4.

Before we explore the breadth of CSM, we will outline the reasons for and the approach to delving deeper into understanding of the content of analysis. In the basic method, we introduced the concept of the "extreme outcome", applying it to exploration of the broad outcomes of the factors that were identified through clustering driving forces in order to "frame" our set of scenario storylines (Stage 6, p. 39). Where a scenario project is carried out over an extended time scale that involves a preparatory period of intensive research and/or multiple iterations of scenario development, the identification of individual driving forces will take place at a level of detail and understanding that does not exist in, say, a one-day exploratory scenario workshop. As a result, it is both possible and desirable to consider the extreme outcomes of individual driving forces, before they are clustered and merged into a smaller number of higher-level factors.

This detailed analysis of driving forces, and its resultant modification of the basic method, is what we now consider.

## AUGMENTED SCENARIO METHOD 1: TOWARDS A DEEPER UNDERSTANDING OF CONTENT

This augmented approach is a modification of the basic method (see Chapter 2), and we outline it with reference to the basic method, as follows.

*   Stage 1: *Setting the Agenda*; and
*   Stage 2: *Determining the Driving Forces* are first undertaken as outlined in Chapter 2 (p. 30).

Following identification and recording of the driving forces, and as the group discusses and agrees a shared meaning for each, members will also discuss and record extreme outcomes for each individual driving force within an **additional stage**, Stage 2b, as follows:

### Stage 2b (Additional): Determining the "Extreme outcomes" – Working as a group

Whilst each driving force is seen to be impacting upon the focal issue and to have an influence on the way its future turns out, the nature of its outcome is likely to vary across different future scenarios. At this point, it is possible to consider the range of these outcomes, in terms of possibility and plausibility. The "limits of the possible" for each driving force are again termed "extreme outcomes". As with cluster outcomes, driving force extreme outcomes are not necessarily defined as at the limits of some continuum – for example, "good/bad". Whilst they may be defined in linear terms, such as good/better, bad/worse, conservative/radical, natural/artificial, and so on, they may also diverge into very different spheres of influence – at one extreme, producing behavioral change in one group of stakeholders; at the other, a financial impact on another. The only rule is that the extremes should be defined creatively to test the limits of thinking, but without breaching the boundaries of possibility and plausibility within the project time horizon.

If this stage is undertaken, each extreme outcome should be recorded on an individual sticky note. Each should be written in as few words as possible, as with the driving forces, but as many as necessary to make it clearly understood in its own right.

*   *Note*: In case of any misunderstanding on the meaning at a later stage, each outcome should be coded in relation to its associate driving force – for example, the extreme outcomes for Driving force no. 74 would be coded 74a and 74b. Whilst it is normal to define extreme outcomes only in terms of two alternative end states, in some cases it may be necessary to outline three possibilities, for this driving force, coded 74a, 74b and 74c (see Figure 5.1).

---

### Example 5.1

A driving force that outlines possible impacts of a particular technology may require that extreme outcomes be described in terms of:

*   existing technology develops and improves;
*   new technology emerges and supplants it; or
*   a non-technological alternative emerges and is adopted.

---

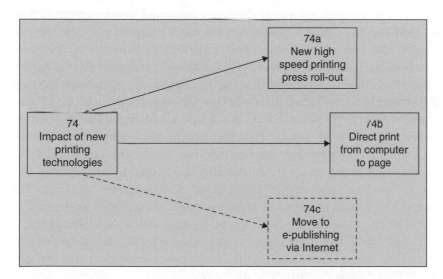

**Figure 5.1** Coding extreme outcomes of individual driving forces

If this stage of augmentation is undertaken, the set of extreme outcomes are set aside following completion of the analysis and are not considered again until they are incorporated into Stage 7: *Scoping the Scenarios* (p. 40). Before moving on, we should say more about how you will use the extreme outcomes at Stage 7. At that point, they provide both a resource both to assist in defining the extreme outcomes of Factors A and B in broader terms than their own component elements, and also add richness to the emergent scenario storylines, through engaging with a broad worldview. If used to define extreme outcomes, they may act as prompts to stretching the imagination, or to "devil's advocate" interrogation of ideas. If adopted to add richness to emergent scenario storylines, particular outcomes may act as stimuli to grasp the attention of parties with a specific interest in the topic, or they may serve as more general prompts to stimulate engagement across a wide audience.

At this point, you should **return to the basic method** framework, as follows:

- Stage 3: *Clustering the Driving Forces*
- **Omit** Stage 4: *Defining the Cluster Outcomes* and move directly to:
- Stage 5: *Impact/Uncertainty Matrix*.
  Having completed Stage 5, you should then undertake a **modified** Stage 6.

## Stage 6b (Alternative): Framing the Scenarios

Where the project approach has not involved implementing Stage 4: *Defining the Cluster Outcomes* for each cluster, you should now undertake the general approach outlined in Stage 4 of the basic method (see Chapter 2), but only for those two higher-level factors identified as Factor A and Factor B. Since the approach you are following here is most likely to be set within an extended time frame project, possibly on a second or third iteration of scenario development, it is likely that the group is dealing with a large amount of very detailed information. As such, the conversation is likely to be much more in-depth and the group to be working with more fine-grained, subtle ideas than in the basic method. This should be borne in mind in terms of time allowances and expectations of the outcomes – both quantity and detail of descriptors.

These detailed descriptors set the overall framing of the scenario storylines that you will now develop, following a **modified** Stage 7 approach, as follows:

## Stage 7b (Alternative): Scoping the Scenarios

Drawing upon the extreme outcomes of Factors A and B (from Stage 6b), and as in Stage 7 of the basic method, you should now consider how the sets of conditions (defined in simplistic terms as bestA1/worstA2 and bestB1/worstB2) interact with each other in the four possible combinations in order to produce what – again, in simplistic terms – might be described as the best/best, best/worst, worst/best and worst/worst (A1/B1, A1/B2, A2/B1 and A2/B2) "worlds" in which the future will unfold. Again, you should brainstorm a very broad range of descriptors of each of these future "worlds", considering what would be the state of society, the economy, technology, national politics, local government, local business, employment, climate, migration, education, crime, transport, cost of living, optimism, pessimism, and so on.

At this stage, in order to add body to the scenario outlines, the group draws upon *all* of the extreme outcomes from each of the driving forces from Stage 2b. This, again, involves critical discussion and debate on relationships of cause and effect, action and outcome, and chronology, since the aim is to place every outcome into the scenario (or scenarios) where it logically sits. Again, as in the basic method, it should be clear that there are relationships between factors that will make some linkages immediately credible and others nonsensical. However, because of the volume and detail of information to be processed, the conversation will be much more intense and prolonged, but the resultant scenario outlines will be much more fine-grained and grounded in "real" events than in a more superficial analysis.

Once the scoping of the scenario outlines is complete, you should return to the basic method.

## Stage 8: Developing the Scenarios is conducted as for the basic method

Again, however, the level of detail and authenticity of the individual scenario stories is likely to be considerably enhanced, due to the greater time and resource input to the project. As a result, it may be that more sophisticated approaches to presentation need to be considered, in order both to maximize the potential of the material, and to create the greatest draw upon the interest of the intended audience.

Whilst it offers a potentially more in-depth analysis of the focal issue, adoption of this more in-depth scenario analysis will be a matter of consideration of the complexity of the issue, the knowledge of the participants, and the time and resources available.

We now outline the second augmented approach.

## AUGMENTED SCENARIO METHOD 2: TOWARDS A BROADER UNDERSTANDING OF IMPACT

The augmented scenario approach that we now outline involves extension of the analytic content of a project. This extension is undertaken **in addition to** either the basic method, from Chapter 2, or the in-depth augmented model outlined here. Whichever foundation approach is followed, scenario method that follows is focused on exploring the limits of possibility and plausibility for the impacts of decision-making with consideration of the "broad" range of stakeholders: "(a)ny identifiable group or individual who can affect the achievement of an organization's objectives or who is *affected* by the achievement of an organization's objectives" (Freeman and Reed, 1983: 91) (emphasis added).

Whilst introducing stakeholder analysis can simply expand the analytic content of a basic scenario approach, here we develop it as a contributor to the CSM (Cairns *et al.*, 2010). CSM focuses thinking on those stakeholders who are not directly involved, who may not be immediately recognized, but who may be deeply affected by the actions of key actors, both now and in future. It involves consideration of moral/ethical issues, the nature and impact of power relationships, and of who are "winners" and "losers" under particular future scenario conditions. The aim of CSM is to enable decision-makers to make more informed judgments about the impact of their decisions, in the hope that they will be prompted to think of their own role in terms of what constitutes a mode of critically-informed "responsible management", rather than a model of mere "compliance management". We would assert that the latter has formed the basis for most management thinking in recent decades. This thinking is based upon a firm-focused view of management and the search for "competitive advantage" (Porter, 1985) through exploitation of opportunity and resources, and is bounded by economic rationality and concepts of "efficiency" and "bottom line" thinking.

This pursuit of the firm's interests in an ever-more competitive business environment is now questioned in light of corporate governance failures in the likes of Enron, WorldCom and Parmalat at the start of the twenty-first century, more recent technological and human error in the Deepwater Horizon collapse, and the overarching impacts of the global financial crisis. Many, not only those within "fringe" groups and environmental organizations, see the need for models of management and organization that address broader social and environmental concerns, and that take account of future legacies from current decisions and actions. This is the realm into which CSM will take you. We first described and illustrated CSM, together with our colleague Martyna Śliwa (Cairns *et al.*, 2010), in a special issue of the journal *Futures*, in which we proposed it as an approach to international business (IB) education in which students would engage with case studies of "success" outlined in major IB textbooks from the perspectives of a full range of stakeholders.

We discussed the example of a global design and supply chain for flat-panel televisions, in which the firm's interests dominated, and broadened it out to bring in consideration of other stakeholders:

- those who produce component parts of the panel screens;
- those whose jobs in manufacturing cathode ray tube (CRT) screens were lost;
- those certified safe recyclers of CRT screens in countries like Singapore;
- those that burn them in conditions of high risk in order extract copper and other materials, in countries like China;
- and those future generations that might be impacted by the effects of higher energy consumption as consumers "upsize" from small CRT televisions to mammoth wall-mounted home cinema units.

The basic steps in undertaking CSM are, as we have outlined, similar to either the basic method or the first augmented method. The variations from these take two forms. First, there is a detailed investigation of who constitute the "broad" stakeholder group in relation to the focal issue or critical uncertainty that we are investigating.

Before we show the detailed stages of stakeholder analysis, we would point out that it can be usefully implemented either near the beginning of a project, as a new and additional Stage 1b, or towards the end, as a new and additional Stage 7c: it can also be incorporated at both stages, if desired. Where it is conducted early in the process, it can be used to assist in the stage of "problem seeking" – defining the key focal issue more clearly:

- Who are the key players (those with both power over and interest in the situation)?
- What concerns them?
- How do these concerns relate to other stakeholders?

Employed at the end of the process, it can be used as a tool for interrogating the logic of developed scenarios:

- Who has high levels of power and interest in each?
- How would they exercise this power?
- Would they really do what the scenario says?

At any stage in the scenario process, stakeholder analysis can also be employed in order to promote the form of engagement through role play that we discuss in Chapter 3:

- Can I put myself in the shoes of this stakeholder?
- Can I empathize with her/his/their concerns and priorities?
- Does this give me a new understanding of my own perspective, my beliefs and my values?

This latter group of questions – engaging with different stakeholders' beliefs and values and their perspectives on what might be "good" or "bad" in different scenarios – takes us into the CSM analysis framework. This draws upon Flybjerg's (2003) set of value-rational questions (see Chapter 4). Before we outline the stages of CSM, let us cover the basic stakeholder analysis.

## Stage 1b and/or Stage 7c (Additional): Stakeholder analysis

As outlined, stakeholder analysis can be used in a number of ways to inform thinking at various stages of the scenario process – in particular, when using the "broad" stakeholder perspective. In considering the broad view of stakeholders in relation to the issue at hand, you should take account of not only of those with direct financial, employment or benefit interests – those who can affect the focal issue through their actions. You should also identify and take account of those who have no effect on the situation, but who may be impacted or affected by its outcomes, both now and in the future,.

Stakeholder groupings can be defined in generic terms, such as "management", "customers" and "media". However, in order to engage meaningfully with stakeholder issues, it is necessary to think about sub-divisions within such groupings. In doing this, you will uncover those sub-groups who will have particular interests and different levels of power.

---

**Example 5.2**

The stakeholder group called "management" might include:

- CEOs with wide-ranging power;
- business unit managers with strategic and operational responsibilities within their defined unit; and
- line managers with local operational responsibility, but with limited strategic influence.

Similarly, "media" might include:

- national television;
- regional radio; and
- local newspapers.

In both examples, the sub-groups have very different (and varying) levels of interest and power.

---

The power/interest matrix (Figure 5.2) promotes consideration of the level of interest different stakeholders' have in what happens, and their degree of power to influence the situation. Discussion should be constructed around joint consideration of who the various stakeholders are, and where they lie within the matrix at a given point in time. It is probably best to start with the present time as the context for this, so that issues of power and interest can be discussed in relation to what is currently known. Critical debate on these key dimensions of stakeholder analysis will often prompt sub-division of categories, as in Example 5.2, where categories such as "management" are seen not to be an all-inclusive group who have both interest in and power over a situation.

At later stages of the scenario development process, stakeholder analysis enables the logic of the emergent scenario storylines to be questioned in several ways. First, it prompts consideration of whether the actions and events that they include are driven by a

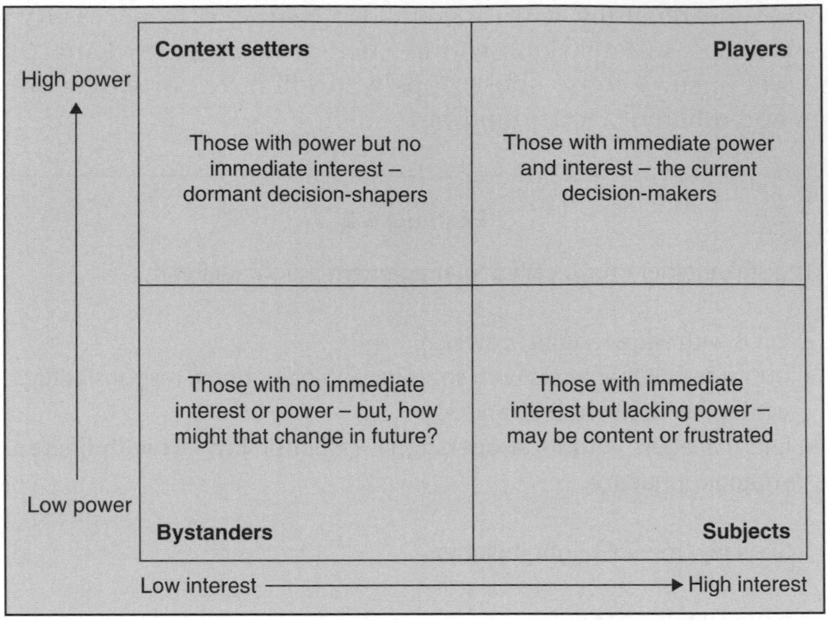

| Context setters | Players |
|---|---|
| Those with power but no immediate interest – dormant decision-shapers | Those with immediate power and interest – the current decision-makers |
| Those with no immediate interest or power – but, how might that change in future? | Those with immediate interest but lacking power – may be content or frustrated |
| Bystanders | Subjects |

High power

Low power

Low interest ⟶ High interest

**Figure 5.2** Stakeholder analysis matrix

rational intuitive view of what is plausible, or are influenced by an emotional response to the problem at hand.

---

**Example 5.3**

MBA students in the UK addressing the issue of "Futures for sustainable health care and education in Sub-Sahara Africa" tended to write in "children" as key stakeholders with an active, rather than a passive involvement in the story. However, when the power dimension was considered, the first approach was seen as being unrealistic and to be based on emotion rather than intuitive logic.

---

Second, it is important to consider how power and interest may shift over time, and across different scenarios.

---

**Example 5.4**

It may be that particular events, such as a hostile takeover or a Presidential election, lead to a change in those stakeholders who constitute the "player" set. On the other hand, it is possible that the existing "players" may take action that leads to change in the status of other stakeholders.

In pondering the possibilities, you should also consider how different stakeholder groups might interact with one another under different sets of conditions, and how this might bring about a step-change in the direction in which a scenario storyline is flowing (see Figure 5.3).

---

**Example 5.5**

You might usefully consider whether a particular radical course of action by current decision-makers ("players") might provoke negative responses from dormant "context setters". Such a move might prompt them to action to challenge the change in order to protect their interests. However, such a situation might also provide ammunition for power-seeking "subjects". Is it possible and plausible to contemplate an alliance between these two groups to resist proposed change? If this happens, these players should beware the consequences!

---

Moving forward from basic stakeholder analysis, we encourage you to consider broader issues of the implications and impact of scenarios for society at large – for the environment, and for future

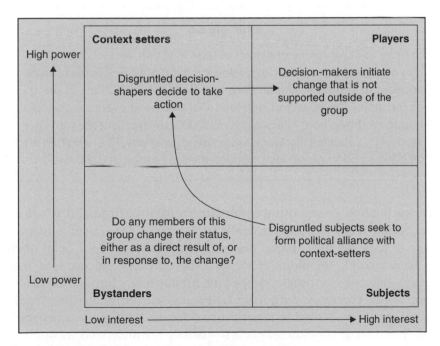

**Figure 5.3** Stakeholder power and politics at work

generations – through seeking engagement with their beliefs, values and concerns within the critical scenario method framework.

## Stage 9 (Additional): Engaging with critical scenario method

We introduced CSM in Chapter 4 as an approach that makes issues transparent and opens them up to exposure where they dominate management decision-making: issues such as short-termism, resource depletion, exploitation of people, and so on. However, it is our hope that such transparency and exposure will not become merely a tool to inform protest and reaction from disaffected groups. It is our sincere hope that CSM will be adopted as a management approach that prompts and supports a new form of "responsible management" (UN Global Compact, 2007) that takes organizations beyond narrow profit maximization and stockholder-value foci. Certainly, our own engagement with senior managers in a broad range of private, public and not-for-profit organizations indicates a growing interest in, and desire for, such management support frameworks in the aftermath of a plethora of failures of governance and accountability.

---

**Example 5.6**

In order to illustrate the principles of CSM in action, we will discuss how it might have been applied in considering alternative responses to those adopted at the time by politicians and financial institutions in the US as the global financial crisis unfolded. Our outline of events as they did happen is drawn from Alfaro and Kim's (2009/10) excellent Harvard Case Study, *U.S. Subprime Mortgage Crisis: Policy Reactions (B)*. Thereafter, we will discuss other possibilities through the application of CSM.

---

The published case summarizes the unfolding financial crisis in the period from September 2008 to March 2009 – over one year after it took its first major toll and long before it had been seen as understood, let alone resolved. The authors' account of this period tells of seemingly desperate measures, changes of direction, about-turns on corporate bail-outs, and critical uncertainty questions that seemed to remain unaddressed, let alone answered. The five-month timeline of events – neatly summarized as such in the Appendix to the published article – covers the period in which newly-elected President Barack Obama took office and pushed Congress to approve a massive US$787 billion stimulus package. In their introduction, the case authors raise important questions that faced the Obama administration in doing this:

> Would the various rescue plans work? What really had to be done to tackle the battered financial system, whose troubles had originated with the subprime mortgage crisis that broke out in 2007? What were the short- and long-term consequences of the new stimulus measures, which were provoking fierce debate about rising nationalism and protectionism? (Alfaro and Kim, 2009/10).

No simple answers are offered to these questions. Rather, the case describes a series of unresolved conflicts around them. There are conflicts between stakeholders in relation to what they think should be done. Some commentators promoted the cause of nationalization, particularly in relation to failing banks. Others, however, argued that this was anathema in a country that espoused free-market capitalism and *laissez-faire* economics. There was also a conflict of reasoning in relation to what was done. The government at one point actively promoted and supported the rescue of the investment bank Bear Stearns. Later, it allowed the demise of Lehman Brothers without intervention. In between, and only a week before Lehman's fall from grace, the Treasury had effectively nationalized two of the US's biggest mortgage lenders, Fannie Mae and Freddie Mac. Finally, there was conflict in terms of the outcomes of the Bush administration's second stimulus package and the intent behind it. Designed to kick-start the economy by promoting consumption, less than 40 percent of the money was actually spent, the rest going to paying off debt and into savings accounts. Overall, the written case sets out a tale of seemingly haphazard decision-making and a lack of consideration of the full range of possible plausible outcomes from action. The authors end their text as they began, with questions: Would the latest economic measure work? How high would US unemployment rise? When would the US economy pull out of a recession that had had world-wide impacts?

The application of scenario thinking, as we have outlined it so far, by financiers, policy-makers, industrialists and others – preferably working together – would not necessarily have avoided the global financial crisis: that would be an arrogant claim with strong hind-sight bias. However, we would argue that it would have supported analysis of the situation, together with other critical questions, through consideration of the driving forces that lay behind them: consideration of the different possible and plausible outcomes that might emerge from them, and of the interrelationship between them in the broad business environment. More specifically, we suggest that the application of CSM enables us to expose and question broader issues of what structural problems lay behind the global financial crisis: what might be the unintended and undesirable consequences of these, what could and should have been done about these, and who would be overall winners and losers under different sets of scenario conditions. We would be bold enough to assert that the application of CSM to complex problems as a matter of course, in a context of active involvement by the full range of stakehold-ers, would make decision-making more overt and explicit, and would decrease the chances of bad decisions being made – or good decisions not being made.

Central to the CSM approach is the set of four value-rational questions of Danish academic Bent Flyvbjerg (2003: 364), to which we referred earlier:

- Where are we going?
- Is this development desirable?
- What, if anything, should we do about it?
- Who gains and who loses, and by which mechanisms of power?

These are applied sequentially in order to interrogate each of the scenarios individually; to enable cross-scenario comparison of their social, economic and environmental implications; and to surface issues of who are the "winners" and who the "losers" within each.

In relation to the global financial crisis example, our start-ing scenario is that set out in the case study text. In relation to the "reality" of the global financial crisis and its origins, the first question – Where are we going? – prompts critical reflection on contemporary society and its institutions. The writer and former senior executive of UBS, Mark Roeder asserts that the global finan-cial crisis arose from the influence of "big mo" – the destructive momentum of a financial system in which its ever-increasing mass and its ever-greater velocity (or speed of transaction) were, by-and-large, beyond human understanding, let alone control (Roeder, 2010). This momentum was grounded in a misplaced belief that economic (and other "natural") forces push towards equilibrium, rather than into acceleration towards, in this case, a destructive extreme. However, he also discusses two points that are of direct relevance to our argument. First, he states that, as early as the first quarter of 2007, some senior analysts were expressing concern about the US subprime housing sector. It was assumed, however, that the problem would be dealt with by some form of "quarantine" and would simply go away. Second, he outlines the need for "friction" forces to restrain negative momentum, and also for active forces to reinforce positive momentum.

We would suggest that a more critical engagement with "where we were going" with the subprime mortgage agenda – pulling in a broad range of involved expert and externally affected stakeholders, in order to analyze the underlying driving forces and their possible and plausible impacts and outcomes – would have surfaced alternative scenarios to that which was blindly accepted by highly intelligent bankers. These alternative scenarios should, of course, have been generated within a scenario exercise undertaken before so many of the world's biggest financial institutions became inescapably linked into the subprime crisis. But, that is another consideration. Each of these scenarios, assuming alternatives would have questioned the rationality of the subprime option, would have generated a very different set of answers, from different stakeholders, to the question: "Is this desirable?" The answers to this question will not always be obvious, and will require committed and critical engagement with the subject. For example, in 2006 – before the first signs of the global financial crisis had emerged openly – the answer to the second question from a low-paid US worker seeking to buy his or her first home would likely be "Yes". But, for many, if not most, that would not be the case two years later. Similarly, for the finance high-flyers whose multi-million dollar bonuses depended upon continuing growth in the housing market, the answer would also be "Yes". For some, who have survived the global financial crisis with government bail-outs and further bonuses, the answer may still be "Yes!"

In relation to those that fall within the final group, the answers to the third and fourth questions are most telling. For them, the answer to what, if anything, we should do about it is possibly

"Nothing". However, their status in retaining their wealth and property – as others have been bankrupted, made homeless and lost their jobs – is revealed by critical debate on the nature of the fourth question: "Who wins and who loses, and by which mechanisms of power?".

In order to illustrate how the full set of questions should be applied in conjunction with stakeholder analysis to support comprehensive engagement with the issue at hand, let us return to the Harvard text. At one point, the authors discuss the call for a "Buy American" policy provision within stimulus funding. Whilst some legislators and the US steel industry – set to be a major beneficiary – did not consider it as such, it was seen by others as being protectionist and risking a trade war backlash from other countries. Consideration of such policy proposals within the CSM framework would prompt debate on the range of possible and plausible impacts in relation to all involved stakeholders. These would include the short- and longer-term impacts on, for example, employment at the local level, the strength of the domestic industry, consumers in terms of choice and price, the nation and its wider interests, other nations across the globe and, their industries and their workforces.

---

**Example 5.7**

In a scenario of protectionism, declining international trade, lack of export markets to the US and global economic stagnation or decline, what would be the impact of a "Buy American" policy on Chinese domestic appliance producers? How might it affect companies' markets and viability? What might be the impact on Chinese workers in this industry, their employment and their families? What might be the knock-on effects of political and economic responses on, say, Boeing's export of aircraft in competition with Airbus? (As an aside, in the contemporary world of transnational enterprises and global supply chains, the question of what is "American", or "British" or "Japanese" is often difficult, if not impossible to answer in relation to a product or service.)

---

In their paper on the CSM, Cairns *et al.* (2010) develop a matrix format in which four scenarios can be interrogated using Flyvbjerg's questions in relation to the full set of stakeholders identified as being involved in or affected by the issue under consideration. Here (Figure 5.4), we show an adaptation of this matrix, with some illustrative examples of content in relation to the global financial crisis scenarios that we have considered. We offer titles for two possible scenarios, both of which take the existence of the global financial crisis for granted. One (A2/B1), along the lines of what has emerged, sets the response to the crisis in terms of, by-and-large, global action in which local responses have been designed with consideration of their wider impacts. The other (A2/B2) posits a global financial crisis that is met with responses of national-ism and protectionism, which would lead to a very different set of outcomes globally.

| Scenario Involved/affected actors | A1/B1 | A2/B1 "GFC and open markets" | A2/B1 | A2/B2 "GFC with recourse to protection" |
|---|---|---|---|---|
| | Where are we going? Is this development desirable? | | | |
| US financial institutions | i) impact ii) response | i) impact ii) response | i) impact ii) response | i) impact ii) response |
| US Treasury | i) impact ii) response | i) impact ii) response | i) impact ii) response | i) ii) |
| US administration | i) impact ii) response | i) impact ii) response | i) ii) | i) ii) |
| Subprime mortgagees | i) impact ii) response | i) ii) | Ftc. | |
| Etc. | | | | |
| Chinese steel manufacturers | | | | |
| Chinese steel workers | | | | |
| Etc. | | | | |
| European banks | | | | |
| Media – local, national and international | | | | |
| Who are the winners? Who are the losers? Who holds power and how do they exercise it? | ?? ?? ?? | ?? ?? ?? | ?? ?? ?? | ?? ?? ?? |

**Figure 5.4** Critical scenario analysis: application of Flyvbjerg's question framework

If this exercise were conducted with foresight, as a scenario project should be, rather than hindsight, the other two options (A1/B1 and A2/B1) would be completed by scenarios in which there was no global crisis, but in which there was either an "open market" world or recourse to "protectionism". Down the left-hand column, we list but a few of the stakeholders that would be relevant to this exercise. In addition to some of which we have spoken, we list "media" at the foot, differentiating local, national and international levels. In the contemporary world of instant communication, global reporting and social networking – where the medium is the message, it is all too easy to forget the power of the media, and their ability to impact situations, and public perception and opinion. We list them in Figure 5.4 in order to ensure that you do not ignore them.

The matrix shows how the first two questions on direction and desirability are answered for each stakeholder group separately in relation to each scenario. Thereafter, the final question on winners, losers and power mechanisms is debated for each scenario, but considering stakeholders in relation to each other. The third question – "What, if anything, should we do about it?" – sits at the crux of CSM. This is where decision-makers must expose their values and their ethics to self-reflection and, if the project is carried out in line with our approach, to the questioning and possible challenge of others. It is our hope that we can promote more considered decision-making by those with power and influence to impact the future state of society and the environment. However, we are happy to expose "bad" decisions to informed critique and resistance, if the interests of the many, and of future generations, are being subordinated to short-term benefits for the few.

## SUMMARY

In this chapter, we have extended the basic scenario method of Chapter 2 in order to promote:

- a greater depth of understanding of complex and ambiguous problems through more focused analysis of its component parts; and

- greater breadth of consideration of impacts and implications of different possible scenarios through incorporation of stakeholder analysis and the adoption of CSM.

In order to gain a greater depth of understanding of how complex problems are defined and understood, we have suggested that, rather than undertaking clustering of driving forces first, then considering the range of possible and plausible outcomes to each cluster group, it is possible to debate and agree the extreme outcomes for individual driving forces. This is a time-consuming exercise and is not one that we would support within a "short, sharp" scenario project, or one that is largely exploratory. We suggest that this approach is most appropriately used where a scenario project is run over an extended period and through multiple iterations, whereby the debate on individual driving forces is underpinned by a detailed knowledge of their nature, context and boundaries, and is informed by any necessary research to enable and support such detailed consideration.

The introduction of stakeholder analysis as an integral part of the scenario process is intended to ensure that thinking within a project is not confined to – or constrained by – consideration of the interests of only those with direct involvement. The "broad" stakeholder approach takes our thinking beyond only those who can directly impact the situation and those who will be immediately affected. It challenges us to consider third parties and beyond: those who may lie at the end of a long chain of cause and effect, and of whom we may not even be aware at the outset; and those who may be impacted in the future by decisions that are taken in the present. Application of the power/interest matrix allows us to consider not only who the obvious decision-makers are, but also who might be alternative power-brokers if their dormant interest in business-as-usual is aroused and converted to active interest under some other scenario conditions. Finally, it enables us to identify those stakeholders with high levels of interest in a situation, but who lack power. This has two key implications. First, it can alert us to possible political activity, whereby disempowered "subjects" might try to unite with disaffected "context setters" in order to challenge the status of current "players". Second, it has the potential to alert us to genuinely disadvantaged subjects whose interests are ignored at present.

In relation to the last group of stakeholders, the introduction of CSM provides a vehicle for consideration of issues of "winners" and "losers" within different scenarios through interrogation of their trajectory, and of the desirability or otherwise of their outcomes for different groups. It enables us to compare and contrast alternative forms of action within various scenarios and requires us to address the issue of power – who holds it, how they use it, and what impact it has on others.

# CHAPTER 6

# Scenarios and Decision Analysis

Until now, we have described how an organization's business idea or strategies can be evaluated against the constructed scenarios of four plausible futures. Our process of evaluation has been relatively informal – a simple allocation of ticks and crosses to give a rough sense of the performance of a particular strategy against a particular scenario. Can we do better than this?

Research on the psychology of decision-making has shown that such global evaluations do not necessarily capture our true view of the worth of an outcome. We tend to choose by focusing on the most important attribute. For example, when considering alternative strategies, we may believe that short-term profit is the most important attribute and therefore choose a strategy that seems to offer the most. If two strategies tie on the most important attribute, then we will tend to turn our attention to the next most important attribute, perhaps market share – and the strategy that scores most on this will tend to be our choice. In technical terms, this has been called a *lexicographic decision principle* – so-called because it resembles a dictionary-like ordering. Another way of simplifying our holistic choices is to focus on the most important attribute and identify a cut-off point that defines the boundary of acceptability. Here, strategies that fail to deliver enough in terms of short–term profit will be eliminated from further consideration. The decision-maker then considers the next-most-important attribute and, in turn, eliminates, say, those strategies that may be acceptable in terms of short-term profit, but fail to deliver in terms of market share. This decision principle is called *elimination by aspects*. Note that both decision principles involve a serial process that is non-compensatory, in that strong performance on market share cannot compensate for poor performance on short-term profit. Note also that each of the two decision principles is easy to explain and justify to others. The former decision principle, based on inclusion, could be justified by: "The two top strategies both promised strong short-term profits, but one also promised a stronger market share." The latter decision principle, based on exclusion, could be justified by: "The two worst strategies promised poor short-term profit and another, whilst strong on short-term profit, promised little in terms of market share."

However, researchers have also shown that the first decision (that of choosing a strategy) and the second decision (that of rejecting strategies) can result in different final choices. Imagine that you are involved in the human resource function of a firm. Would the task of selecting only those job applicants to take forward for further consideration result in a different set of applicants than choosing only those applicants to exclude from any further consideration? Research has shown that following the former strategy of inclusion leaves less of the initial alternatives under subsequent consideration than the latter strategy of exclusion. Also, the strategy of inclusion leads to a more extensive search – to see how well a candidate performs on the multiple attributes that are important in the selector's evaluation process. By contrast, a strategy of exclusion results in a more cursory evaluation of those candidates that are rejected and, perhaps in recognition of this more-superficial evaluation, more candidates are included for further subsequent consideration. Both decision principles are also easy on our mental capabilities – once an alternative (e.g. candidate for a job, strategic option) is considered and then dismissed, there is no need to think about it again. Once it's gone, it's gone.

Research has also shown that the degree to which attributes are shared across alternatives influences which alternatives are preferred. For example, if a decision-maker knows the leg-room of a range of airlines' economy-class seating, then information on this attribute is shared. Conversely, if the leg-room for only one airline's seating is known, then the attribute information is unique. Decision-makers tend to place more importance on attributes that possess unique rather than shared information.

But such ways of making choices seem intuitively limited. It would seem preferable to take into account all attributes – one of which may be perceived as more important than the others, and also to trade off how well an option does on one of the attributes against how well it does on the other. This *compensatory* approach is the essence of the decision analysis approach to strategy evaluation against scenarios, which we will now introduce in a more formal way. We will also give clear, step-by-step guidelines on how to use this approach in scenario method.

## COMBINING SCENARIO THINKING AND DECISION ANALYSIS

In scenario practice, evaluation of strategies against the decision-maker's strategic objectives is relatively informal. As we have discussed, when a number of objectives are involved, there are dangers in this informal process. Strategy evaluation may be incomplete or distorted because, unconsciously, undue attention is paid to particular objectives, at the expense of others.

In this chapter, we present one way of formalizing the process of strategy evaluation that draws closely on the work of Goodwin and Wright (2001, 2009), who first developed a systematic method to aid the process of evaluating strategies. We believe that the use of the technique can bring considerable advantages to scenario planning. We now present a simplified, less numerical version of their approach.

The main stages of the approach are:

- Stage 1: Formulate scenarios;
- Stage 2: Formulate the objectives that you wish to achieve in your strategic actions;
- Stage 3: Design alternative strategies;
- Stage 4: For each objective, rank each strategy against each scenario from the best to the worst;
- Stage 5: For each objective, rank all strategy–scenario combinations from best to worst;
- Stage 6: Compute the sum-of-ranks for each strategy and provisionally select the best performing strategy.

---

### Example 6.1

Our case study concerns a small but well-accredited business school that is based in the UK. It has a strong UK-origin undergraduate program and also does quite well in attracting students from across the world to its Masters programs. It has a complement of strong national academics with a substantial number of non-UK origin ex-PhD students who have taken up assistant professor positions at the business school.

---

## STAGE 1: FORMULATE SCENARIOS

For simplicity, only two short scenarios will be used here:

### Scenario 1: The rise of Internet business schools (Internet)

In this scenario, video-conferencing and Internet-based technologies advance such that anyone, anywhere, is able to view talks by distinguished academics from across the world almost as though they were in the lecture room. Several well-known business schools have contracted world-famous academics to deliver lectures and also to deliver short video clips that respond, quite precisely, to the questions that audience members often ask. Other less-well-known academics deliver online tutorials that also give a near face-to-face user experience.

### Scenario 2: Academic migration takes off (Migration)

In this scenario, most business school courses are taught in the English language, no matter where in the world a course is taught. Those academics with English language skills who are also strong researchers can find jobs anywhere in a booming sector. Some business schools pay what is necessary to attract the best staff, and there is a polarization of business schools in Europe and the World – that is, world-class business schools and also-rans.

## STAGE 2: FORMULATE THE OBJECTIVES THAT YOU WISH TO ACHIEVE IN YOUR STRATEGIC ACTIONS

The five objectives identified by the management team are to maximize:

- the market share of the international student market
- the satisfaction of local students who reside within the business school's physical catchment area
- monetary surplus over the medium to long term
- the intellectual environment necessary for strong academic research activity.

## STAGE 3: DESIGN ALTERNATIVE STRATEGIES

Here are three alternative strategies:

- Invest to develop an IT-enhanced distance learning provision (DISTANCE);
- Invest to attract top UK-based academics to work at the business school (UK ACADEMIC);
- Partner with other European business schools to offer a multi-centre experience for students (MULTI-CENTER).

In our simplified example, we assume that the three strategies are mutually exclusive of one another because of resource constraints: there is only funding available to pursue one of the three strategies. In reality, mixed strategies will also be options for consideration and analysis.

## STAGE 4: FOR EACH OBJECTIVE, RANK EACH STRATEGY AGAINST EACH SCENARIO FROM BEST TO WORST

The ranks within each of the four objectives are given in Examples 6.2 to 6.5. In our simplified example, there are only two scenarios, and so the best performance of a particular strategy is ranked as "1" and the worst performance is ranked as "2".

**Example 6.2**

**Objective: Maximize market share of the international student market**

| | Scenario | |
| Strategy | INTERNET | MIGRATION |
| --- | --- | --- |
| DISTANCE | 1 | 2 |
| UK ACADEMIC | 2 | 1 |
| MULTI-CENTER | 2 | 1 |

Thus, in terms of attracting international students, investment in IT-enhanced distance learning provision does better under the "rise of the Internet business schools" scenario (INTERNET) than under the "academic migration takes off" scenario (MIGRATION). Under INTERNET, the business school will be equipped to deploy its resident academic expertise across the world. Under MIGRA-TION, such an IT investment will be of little use if the business school's resident academics start to leave for better-paid jobs elsewhere.

By contrast, investment by the business school in attracting top UK-academics to re-locate to the business school will perform less well in INTERNET, where the Internet-based business schools prosper, than in MIGRATION, where UK academics are offered high pay at other business schools.

Finally, it is felt by the management team that investment in multi-center partnerships with other European business schools will, to a degree, perform better under MIGRATION than INTERNET.

We now move on to consider the second objective: maximizing the satisfaction of locally-based students with the business school's academic offerings. For example, a strategy of investing in IT-based distance learning was viewed as better satisfying the locally-based students when other business schools were promoting their distance learning offerings than in the scenario where the business school was making a similar investment but, at the same time, losing its core complement of strong English-speaking academics to better-paid jobs elsewhere in Europe and the World. After some thought and discussion, the rankings as given in Example 6.3 were seen as appropriate by the management team.

### Example 6.3

**Objective: Maximize satisfaction of local students within the business school's physical catchment area**

|  | Scenario | |
| --- | --- | --- |
| Strategy | INTERNET | MIGRATION |
| DISTANCE | 1 | 2 |
| UK ACADEMIC | 2 | 1 |
| MULTI-CENTER | 1 | 2 |

For the final two objectives – maximizing surplus, and maximizing the intellectual environment of the business school – the management team developed the rankings given in Examples 6.4 and 6.5.

## Example 6.4

**Objective: Maximize surplus over the medium to long term**

| | Scenario | |
| --- | --- | --- |
| Strategy | INTERNET | MIGRATION |
| DISTANCE | 1 | 2 |
| UK ACADEMIC | 2 | 1 |
| MULTI-CENTER | 1 | 2 |

## Example 6.5

**Objective: Maximize the intellectual environment for the academics' research activity**

| | Scenario | |
| --- | --- | --- |
| Strategy | INTERNET | MIGRATION |
| DISTANCE | 1 | 2 |
| UK ACADEMIC | 2 | 1 |
| MULTI-CENTER | 2 | 1 |

# STAGE 5: FOR EACH OBJECTIVE, RANK ALL STRATEGY–SCENARIO COMBINATIONS FROM BEST TO WORST

Now we have evaluated the strategies on a single objective within each scenario, but the performance of the best strategy under one scenario might be nowhere near as good as the performance of the best strategy under another of the scenarios. This means that we now need to compare the performances of the strategies across scenarios. After the completion of Stage 4, a further, more detailed ranking of the six strategy/scenario combinations from 1 to 6 can now be more easily developed for each of the management team's objectives. This is best achieved with an intermediate sub-ranking, by rank-ordering all the "1" ranks (in our case, from i to iii) and then rank-ordering all the "2" ranks (in our case, also, from i to iii). This sub-ranking produced by the management team for the objective of maximizing market share is illustrated in Example 6.6. Thus, "1i" denotes what the management team views as the highest-ranked strategy/scenario combination for maximizing market share. "1ii" denotes what is viewed as the second-highest-ranked combination, "1iii" the third, and "2i" the fourth, and so on.

**Example 6.6**

**Objective: Maximize market share of the international student market**

| | Scenario | |
| --- | --- | --- |
| Strategy | INTERNET | MIGRATION |
| DISTANCE | 1i | 2ii |
| UK ACADEMIC | 2i | 1iii |
| MULTI-CENTER | 2iii | 1ii |

Thus, investing in distance learning is thought to produce the highest market share of international students, if the rise of the Internet business schools scenario prevails. By contrast, the worst market share is thought to be the outcome if the business school devotes its investment to building multi-center collaborations in the scenario of strong Internet-based business school offerings to these international students. Obviously there will be a great deal of debate in the management team about the rank ordering of the outcomes of the strategy/scenario combinations. A key check on the process is to confirm that "1iii" has, in the scenario team's view, a higher ranking than that of "2i". If it has, then proceed. If it hasn't, then consider switching the overall rankings. In our case, 1iii and 2i are both attached to the same strategy against our two scenario combinations, and so it follows that our overall ranking of "1iii" will, logically, be higher than that for "2i", since we made this evaluation at an earlier stage.

Within our example, our management team's rankings of individual strategies against the scenarios for the objective of maximizing market share, achieved at Stage 4, convert to the 1 to 6 rank ordering *across* all strategy/scenario combinations within the objective of maximizing market share of the international student market (Example 6.7).

**Example 6.7**

**Objective: Maximize market share of the international student market**

| Strategy | Scenario | |
|---|---|---|
|  | *INTERNET* | *MIGRATION* |
| DISTANCE | 1 | 5 |
| UK ACADEMIC | 4 | 3 |
| MULTI-CENTER | 6 | 2 |

Moving on, the management team, after debate, agreed the following rankings across strategy–scenario combinations for the remaining three objectives (Examples 6.8 to 6.10).

**Example 6.8**

**Objective: Maximize satisfaction of local students within the business school's physical catchment area**

| Strategy | Scenario | |
|---|---|---|
|  | *INTERNET* | *MIGRATION* |
| DISTANCE | 2 | 5 |
| UK ACADEMIC | 4 | 1 |
| MULTI-CENTER | 3 | 6 |

**Example 6.9**

**Objective: Maximize monetary surplus over the medium to long term**

| Strategy | Scenario | |
|---|---|---|
|  | *INTERNET* | *MIGRATION* |
| DISTANCE | 2 | 6 |
| UK ACADEMIC | 4 | 1 |
| MULTI-CENTER | 3 | 5 |

**Example 6.10**

**Objective: Maximize the intellectual environment for the academics' research activity**

|  | Scenario | |
| Strategy | INTERNET | MIGRATION |
| --- | --- | --- |
| DISTANCE | 3 | 6 |
| UK ACADEMIC | 4 | 1 |
| MULTI-CENTER | 5 | 2 |

## STAGE 6: COMPUTE THE SUM-OF-RANKS FOR EACH STRATEGY AND PROVISIONALLY SELECT THE BEST-PERFORMING STRATEGY

If we assume that all the objectives carry equal weight, then the sum of ranks attached to each of the strategic options against each of the scenarios is as shown in Example 6.11.

**Example 6.11**

|  | Scenario | |
| Strategy | INTERNET | MIGRATION |
| --- | --- | --- |
| DISTANCE | 8 | 22 |
| UK ACADEMIC | 16 | 6 |
| MULTI-CENTER | 17 | 15 |

This result indicates, very roughly, that the strategy of investing in partnerships with other European business schools is less-favored than the strategy of investing in attracting top UK-based academics to work at the business school. In both scenarios, the former strategy does worse than the latter strategy. Note that the DISTANCE strategy performs better under the INTERNET scenario than under the MIGRATION scenario. Conversely, the UK ACADEMIC strategy performs better under the MIGRATION scenario than under the INTERNET scenario. Thus, each of these two strategies is best suited to a different scenario. No one strategy, in this instance, performs well under all scenarios.

Another way of think about the attractiveness of the alternative strategies is to consider increasing the weight of achieving one strategic objective relative to other objectives. How should the weightings of the strategic objectives be decided? The key is to consider the range over which the rankings of an objective vary. To see this, consider three cars, whose performance in terms of miles per gallon varies between 40 and 45. Choice of the most efficient or least efficient car in this range will not add substantially to the owner's operating costs over a year: if she travels 10,000 miles a year, then the difference in fuel used will only be 38 gallons. But, if one of the cars being considered was a 15-mpg gas-guzzler, then the difference in operating costs would be over 400 additional gallons a year. So, the importance of an objective depends to a large extent on the range over which it varies, and this issue needs to be thought over carefully by the management team. One way forward is to take a short-cut and simply double the impact of an objective that has a range of rankings (worst to best) that appear, after discussion, to be most important. For example, one change could be to double the weighting on maximizing the business school's medium- to long-term monetary surplus. As an indicator of this doubling, the ranks that were agreed for this objective at Stage 5 should be added, once again, to the sum of ranks in Example 6.11. This addition would result in the revised sum of ranks given in Example 6.12.

### Example 6.12

| | Scenario | |
| Strategy | INTERNET | MIGRATION |
| --- | --- | --- |
| DISTANCE | 10 | 28 |
| UK ACADEMIC | 20 | 7 |
| MULTI-CENTER | 20 | 20 |

This revised result indicates that the MULTI-CENTER option is still out-performed by the strategy of investing in attracting top UK-based academics to the business school. Also, the DISTANCE and UK ACADEMIC strategies still remain complements of one another. If we were to increase the weighting on maximizing the business school's monetary surplus to make it equal in weight to the other three objectives combined, then, once again, the ranks that were agreed for this objective at Stage 5 should be added to the sum of ranks. After trebling of the weighting of the objective of maximizing the business school's monetary surplus, the resulting sum of ranks would be as given in Example 6.13. This suggests, still, that the multi-centre campus option is the weakest of the three strategies, and that the remaining two strategies are complements of one other. Note, however, that this method of increasing weightings is sensitive to the number of scenario–strategy combinations. For example, if you have six combinations, the lowest rank will be 6; if you have 30, the lowest rank will be 30, too. Thus, if you have strategies that perform only slightly differently on an objective across the scenarios, then the worst performing strategy–scenario combination would be massively penalized by gaining a rank of 60, or 90, if the ranks are doubled or trebled. For this reason, we recommend that strategies that perform very poorly on particular objectives are given special attention in management team discussions before being omitted from further discussion and consideration.

**Example 6.13**

|            | Scenario | |
| Strategy   | INTERNET | MIGRATION |
| --- | --- | --- |
| DISTANCE     | 12 | 34 |
| UK ACADEMIC  | 24 | 8  |
| MULTI-CENTER | 23 | 25 |

This focus on changing weightings of the objectives is an important stage in the analysis and can serve, after discussion, to reduce the number of strategic options that are being considered. It may also, of course, provide a focus for discussion that will enable a strategy to be modified in some way to avoid its removal from the set of options that subsequently will be given further consideration by the management team. In our case, we will provisionally remove the multi-centre strategy, and focus on the distance learning and academic recruitment strategies.

Note, in example 6.13, that the row-sum-of-ranks for investing in distance learning is 46, whilst the row-sum-of-ranks for investing in attracting UK-based academics to work at the B-school is 32, indicating, provisionally, that the management team should now focus on discussing the advantages and limitations of the latter strategy. Also, of course, it may be that resources can be found to fund both strategies, at least to some degree, and thus provide a degree of robustness against both scenarios. Alternatively, if one strategy is chosen over the other, then the management team should be sensitive to the early-warning signals contained in the unfolding of the early events contained within a scenario that is negative for a particular strategy.

### Example 6.14

| | Scenario | |
| Strategy | INTERNET | MIGRATION |
| --- | --- | --- |
| DISTANCE | 12 | 34 |
| UK ACADEMIC | 24 | 8 |

As we have stressed throughout, the rankings used in our analysis were based on rough-and-ready judgments. Also, in a group of decision-makers there are likely to be differences in opinions or minority views. For these reasons, it can often be useful in practice to investigate the effect of changes in these values on the overall evaluations of particular strategies. Often, the relative performance of strategies is robust to changes in these judgmental inputs. Exploring differences in opinions about relative rankings can lead to the easy resolution of disputes between members of a management team, who, for example, may find that the same strategy is always superior, even though members of the team disagree about some of the constituent rankings.

# CHAPTER 7

# Creating Robust Strategies and Robust Organizations

So far, we have demonstrated how to develop scenarios that describe a range of futures. But, as we have discussed, sometimes the unexpected can happen. Consider the 9/11 attacks on the US homeland. With hindsight, these attacks and the methods used to achieve them seem predictable. Airliner cockpits were, then, relatively insecure and easily accessed by motivated individuals posing as passengers who, once inside the cockpit, had the flying experience necessary to pilot the airliner to a target destination: the Twin Towers, the Pentagon and one other target that was not reached. But US-based newspapers and magazines were mute about such a possibility before its terrible occurrence, despite numerous precursor signals throughout the 1990s, including Al Qaeda's attacks on US embassies in Africa, its thwarted plan to blow up multiple aircraft in flight over the Pacific, and the previous failed attempt to bomb the World Trade Center. The sequence of events and the effect of stakeholder capabilities and motivations on the events of 9/11 appear now to have been obvious, with hindsight – like standing dominoes falling one against the other in an unstoppable sequence. But, before the event, such a sequence was one of many thousands – each, perhaps, equally likely, but yet equally implausible. In this chapter, we discuss biases that can lead to inappropriate confidence in predictions of the likelihood of future events, and then consider what an organization should do both to protect itself against the occurrence of high-impact negative events, and to take advantage of the occurrence of high-impact positive events.

## HINDSIGHT BIAS

In one famous study, Baruch Fischhoff (1975) had MBA students estimate their confidence for the occurrence of then-future events linked to then-President Nixon's forthcoming trip to China. Would a particular treaty be signed? Would a particular Chinese official be met? Would a particular Chinese city be visited? The MBA students made many estimates of such events. Then, two weeks later, after the events had, or had not, happened the students were again in their MBA classroom. Unexpectedly, Dr Fischhoff asked each of the students to consider, once again, each of the events and to try to recall the confidence estimate that they had each originally made two weeks earlier. Fischhoff found that, if a particular named event had occurred, the students tended to recall that they had placed a high confidence on the occurrence. Conversely, if the event had not occurred, then the students tended to recall that they had placed a low confidence level on its occurrence. These recollections showed systematic bias: remembered predictions of the once-future events "moved" toward an event's occurrence (if the event happened) or non-occurrence (if the event had not happened), resulting in what Fischhoff termed the "I-knew-it-all-along" effect.

Such a hindsight bias limits the possibility of improving confidence estimates in the light of experience, and tends to inflate, inappropriately, our confidence in our judgmental forecasting abilities. We feel that we are able to predict the future and, after the event, recall that our predictions were correct. Why are we so confident? We turn to discuss this issue next.

## THE WAITER'S DILEMMA AND CONFIRMATION BIAS

Psychologists have described a common-place decision problem: the so-called the "waiter's dilemma". The waiter's dilemma illustrates some of the problems we will have to overcome to become better intuitive forecasters. Imagine that you are a waiter in a busy restaurant and, because you cannot give good service to all the people who sit at the tables that you serve, you use your judgment to identify those people who will leave good tips or poor tips. You have developed this ability well, and most of the people whom you predict will tip generously do so. Also, most of those that you predict will not tip do not do so. Are your judgmental predictions accurate?

At first sight, it would seem that they are. Most waiters are confident of their ability to spot the good tippers. However, note that the waiter will give good service to those he thinks will tip well, and will ignore those he thinks will not tip. If the quality of service, in itself, has an effect on whether or not a customer tips, then the waiter's actions will, by themselves, determine the tipping outcome.

There is a strong element of a self-fulfilling prophecy here. The only true way that the waiter can test out the quality of this judgment is to give *poor* service to potential good tippers and *excellent* service to potential poor tippers. Clearly, his original judgments could be less valid than he assumes, as he has not accurately tested them. This tendency to invest little effort to testing the true quality of our judgment is called the *confirmation bias.*

In another demonstration of confirmation bias, a class of MBA students is told that we have a rule in mind that classifies sets of three whole numbers, which we call "triples". The class is given an example of a triple that has been produced by our rule: 2, 4, 6. Members of the class attempt to discover the rule by suggesting other triples to test. We say whether the triples that are called out conform to the rule or not. Participants are told not to call out what they think the rule is until they are certain that they have deduced it. Our rule is simply "any ascending sequence of three numbers", but most participants think that the rule is more complex – for example, "ascending in equal intervals" – suggesting triples such as 4, 8, 12 or 20, 40, 60. Eventually, members of the class announce their rule and are convinced of its correctness – but turn out to be wrong. In other words, people tend to think only of positive tests of their view of the rule. They offer a view that can never be falsified: a bias toward confirmation, rather than disconfirmation of our prediction. This result suggests that, without prompting, we are unlikely, as waiters, to give service to those predicted to be poor tippers.

The decision to hire new employees is analogous to the waiter's situation. Most of us feel that we are able to interview fairly, and we feel comfortable with our hiring decisions, confident that we can identify appropriate employees. But we seldom hear what happened to the candidates that we declined. Unless we gain accurate feedback on the future success of the interviewees that we turned down, we do not know whether our decisions were sound. We seldom get such feedback, unless, by accident, we recognize that one person we rejected is now a media megastar – such as Richard Branson. It follows that the only true test of our interviewing capabilities is to hire those that we feel we should reject. But few of us would willingly put our judgment to such rigorous tests.

In short, we are likely to seek confirming evidence that our favored prediction is correct. Inevitably, we do not place ourselves in situations where we can test the quality of our judgment. We only seek information that will confirm the quality of our predictions. For example, we tend to read adverts about the car that we have just purchased rather than those describing the virtues of the cars that we considered and then dismissed before we made our purchase decision. This may seem relatively harmless, but it demonstrates that our minds are psychologically closed to information that may disconfirm our previous decisions and predictions. Tetlock (2005) found that when the predictions of experts turned out to be wrong, the experts explained away their mistakes with justifications such as "the forecast event almost occurred", "OK, the event has not happened yet, but it will", or "my timing was just off".

## WHEN THE UNEXPECTED OCCURS

So, we tend to believe that our judgments and decisions are well-made and, due to the confirmation bias and the hindsight bias, tend to experience little to counter this viewpoint. We feel confident in our judgmental forecasting abilities and this confidence remains unshaken, other than by the occurrence of high-impact rare events that we had not previously considered and the occurrence of which cannot be easily explained away – such as the global financial meltdown of 2008 and the 9/11 attacks on the US homeland. Here, it is clear that even with the diluting effects of hindsight bias, the unexpected happened. The occurrence of other high-impact rare events – such as the fall of the Berlin Wall, the Deepwater Horizon rig disaster, and even the proof that the Titanic was not unsinkable – also provided a sudden jolt to our usual confidence in the quality of our judgmental forecasting abilities.

Taleb (2008) has argued that we tend to think of the movements of the stock market as following a normal distribution, with most movements being small-scale and centered on the average of the distribution. More extreme movements are relatively infrequent, in terms of their historic occurrence. But, the issue is that these historic movements at the extremes are, by definition, relatively rare and their relative rarity gives us little information about their true likelihood of occurrence: and this likelihood may be much greater than historically anticipated. As Taleb noted, the stock market crash of Black Monday, in 1988, represented a fall of 20 standard deviations from the mean and, hence, on the basis of historic information, should only have occurred "every several billion lifetimes of the universe".

Since the occurrence of high-impact rare events cannot be predicted beforehand, what should we do to prepare ourselves and our organizations? One way to plan is to prepare ourselves for all possible eventualities. Imagine that you are a car driver who is planning to drive a thousand miles across the country. A well-prepared driver would carry extra cans of fuel, a comprehensive set of spare parts, another driver – in case he/she gets ill, an onboard mechanic, and a small motorcycle strapped to the back of the car. Such a car journey would be expensive in terms of both fixed and variable costs. On the other hand, the journey would be fairly certain to be completed successfully, since the car and its on-board accessories would enable it to be resistant to the eventualities of most types of breakdown and fuel stations being closed along the route. Taleb (2009) argues for redundancy in financial investment by retaining "idle" capital – so-called de-leveraging. He notes that human beings have some duplicate organs, and also some organs can take on new functions – so-called degeneracy. Thus, maximizing redundancy, although increasing costs and restricting the possibility of leveraging resources, enables survival in difficult times. Makridakis *et al.* (2009) argue that business strategies should be built to the same analogous standard as buildings that are designed to withstand low-probability, but high-impact earthquakes.

An alternative to having strategies to provide protection against unknown events that are assumed to be completely unpredictable is to try to identify all possible high-impact events that might occur and make contingency plans to deal with them For example, in the sphere of crisis management, Pearson and Clair (1998) noted that many organizations prepare for the crisis that they believe most probable, or that will have most impact if it occurs. These authors argue that, instead, "the best-prepared organizations compile a crisis portfolio for an assortment of crises that would demand different responses ... this may seem a wasteful approach but ... the most dangerous crises ... cause greater trouble, specifically because no-one was thinking about or preparing for them" (p. 55). However, the cost–benefit trade-off of preparing an organization for all possible crises is not addressed. Neither is a systematic approach offered to enable managers to rank-order crises for differential attention.

Similar issues are now at the forefront of debate in thinking about climate change and how to prepare for it. It is to this debate that we now turn. We will draw out implications for the design of both strategies and organizations that are able to survive the occurrence of high-impact rare events.

## ORGANIZATIONAL DESIGN: LESSONS FROM CLIMATE-CHANGE RESEARCHERS

How do you protect communities against unexpected weather events?

Wardekker *et al.* (2010) argue that:

- *Resilience* should be a key objective. Roads should be designed to enhance the removal of water from flooding, and urban planning should design building configurations such that wind-flow through an area aids the evaporation of water.
- Communities should also design in *redundancy* – which refers to securing multiple ways for a community to fulfill its needs by, for example, having diversification in energy supplies and transportation methods.
- The planning cycle should be one of *high flux* – where short planning cycles result in the design of buildings to last for 30 years rather than 50 years. Thus, urban areas can be modified more quickly to accommodate change in climatic conditions.
- Community response to climatic events should be based upon in-built organizational *flatness*, having few levels of hierarchy so that early-warning signals are recognized as such, and necessary action taken swiftly. Community members should also have the competence and authority to respond to local events in a self-managed way, and should be self-regulating and self-organizing.
- Buildings should be designed to absorb climatic disturbance by *buffering* – for example, designing in non-essential and flood-resistant functions at ground-level. Functions such as ICTs should be placed on the higher-level floors of the buildings. Also, low-lying areas of cities can be designed as water-retention areas for a limited period until high-tides recede.

Eriksson and Weber (2008) argue for the benefit of *keeping options open* – at least, until they can be used effectively, or we know that the options have become irrelevant – so-called "adaptive and flexible planning". These authors contrast keeping options open with robust strategies that are fixed and static. Robust strategies are passive and protective, whilst keeping options open is dynamic and strategically opportunistic. Eriksson gives an example of preparing for the eventuality of a fire breaking out in one's home. The installation of smoke sensors around the house is a robust protective response, whilst the fire brigade that arrives in response to an automated call from a sensor is, by contrast, able to respond in a flexible and adaptive way to the demands of the actual fire scene. Marchau *et al.* (2010) describe adaptive strategies in an analogous way to a ship's captain guiding a ship through a long ocean voyage. The goal of the destination is set at the beginning of the voyage but, along the way, unpredictable storms and other shipping will interfere with the original planned course, such that on-the-spot course alterations are made to achieve the destination – which, itself, remains unchanged. Overall, a priority should be placed on the *tolerance* and *adaptability* of decisions already made. In the context of climate change, local organizations should be able to respond to location-specific needs, rather than having to respond according to nationally- or regionally defined, more rigid frameworks. Since the areas of responsibilities of organizations based in geographically close areas will overlap, redundancy of resources and capabilities will be prevalent.

All of this provides lessons for strategy development.

## Strategic defense

Strategies should be evaluated for:

- robustness – against the worst eventualities;
- resilience – such that organizational buffering and tolerance are strong so that recovery can be swift; and
- redundancy in the organization's capabilities to protect it against the worst eventualities.

## Strategic opportunism

Strategies should also be evaluated for:

- flexibility in decision-making – such that the organization's response can be adaptable to emerging opportunities and not committed to large-scale previous commitments; and
- flatness of organizational decision-making – such that emerging opportunities are swiftly evaluated and responded to in a decentralized, self-organized, manner

In his book *The Black Swan*, Taleb (2008) was also concerned with the issue of how to cope with the occurrence of high-impact, poorly predictable events. He, too, advocates defense against negative events and exposure to potentially positive events. A few quotations from the book illustrate his stance on a ways of dealing with uncertainty:

> Instead of putting your money on "medium risk " investments ... you need to put a portion, say 85–90%, in extremely safe ... the remaining 10–15% you put in extremely speculative bets ... that way you do not depend on errors of risk management; no black swan can hurt you at all, beyond your "floor". You are clipping the incomputable risk.
> ...
> Instead of having medium risk you have high risk on one side and no risk on the other ... maximum exposure to the positive black swans while remaining paranoid about the negative ones. For your exposure to the positive black swan you do not need any precise understanding of the structure of uncertainty ... The scalability of real-life pay-offs ... makes the pay-off unlimited or of unknown limit.
> ...
> The notion of asymmetric outcomes is the central idea of this book: I will never get to know the unknown since, by definition, it is unknown. However, I can guess how it might affect me, and I should base my decision around that ... in order to make a decision you need to focus on the consequences (which you can know) rather than the probability (which you can't know).

But, of course, there is also an extra dimension that is the focus of this book. Our concern takes us beyond both the concerns of climate change researchers and beyond the idea of black swans. Our focus is that of the usefulness of thinking about multiple scenarios of the future business environment that could, plausibly, face an organization and its strategies. Our attention is thus on a third element of successful strategy development – that of future-orientated thinking. How can scenario thinking be utilized in a systematic way in order to enhance both strategic defense and strategic opportunism? In the next section of this chapter, we develop our answer to this question.

## EVALUATING STRATEGIES AGAINST SCENARIOS

In earlier chapters, we detailed our scenario method and introduced the idea of searching for robust strategies that work well against a range of scenarios. Table 7.1 summarizes an example of how a particular set of strategies might be evaluated against scenarios produced using the approach that we have advocated thus far.

We next use a case study (loosely based on a presentation made by Thomas Amos' MBA scenario group at Durham Business School in 2006) to illustrate our approach to evaluating the degree to which strategic defense and strategic opportunism are inherent in particular strategic options. This case study concerns a high-street retailer who sells clothing, food and a range of household durables. Figure 7.1 represents the firm's business idea. A business idea is the *systemic* linking of the business's competencies and strengths. Here, the *strengths* that the retailer possesses are summarized in short statements. The impact of the deployment of these strengths produces revenue, and the reinvestment of the revenue obtained produces a self-reinforcing cycle or positive feedback loop that would, in a stable environment, be a *robust* business idea that would become less and less replicable by competitors – without serious investment from a competitor over a period of time.

Overall, a business idea should specify three major elements of a business's attempt to be successful:

- the *competitive advantage* that is aimed for – in the case of the high-street retailer, this is a business idea that is differentiated from its competitors;
- the *distinctive competencies* on which competitive advantage is based – for example, an ability to sell high-quality products

**Table 7.1** Evaluation of strategies against scenarios

| Possible strategies | Scenario 1 | Scenario 2 | Scenario 3 | Scenario 4 |
|---|---|---|---|---|
| Strategy 1 | +++ | + | -- | ++ |
| Strategy 2 | + | -- | ++ | - |
| Strategy 3 | -- | +++ | --- | + |
| Robust strategy | +++ | +++ | +++ | +++ |

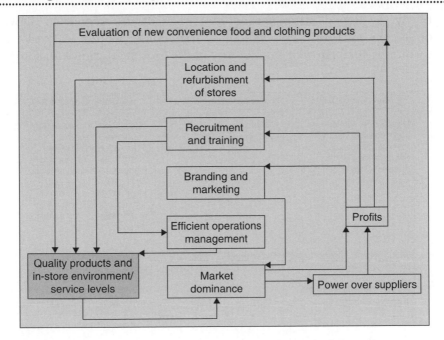

**Figure 7.1** The business idea for the high street retailer

from a high-quality physical in-store shopping environment, coupled with high-quality sales (and after-sales) service to customers; and

• the *growth* mechanism – a positive feedback loop.

Obviously, the retailer's business would be affected by changes in the use of technology for shopping – witness the growth of Internet-based sales of books and electronic goods – and also by the degree to which cheaply-made clothes and cheaply-grown food can be transported across the globe to be sold within its own, and competitors', high-street stores. Figure 7.2 documents possible scenario dimensions and plausible outcomes in the format that we have used in earlier chapters.

The essence of each of the four scenario storylines that were constructed from combinations of the four plausible outcomes is presented in Figures 7.3 to 7.6.

At this point in application of the conventional scenario method, we would then evaluate the current business idea and develop possible strategies for the high-street retailer that could be deployed against the four scenarios. The usual next step in strategy evaluation would be to make an evaluation of each of these newly developed strategies against each of the scenarios. Obviously, the current business idea of the retailer would, in the long-term, not perform well against any of the four scenarios – although,

| Plausible outcome 1 | Possible scenario dimension | Plausible outcome 2 |
|---|---|---|
| Most people continue, or begin, to shop via the Internet because of convenience and cost benefits – they shop less in high street stores | Dimension A:<br>**Shopping with technology** | The steady increase in the popularity and online safety of buying via the Internet leads to very strong competition among retailers, driving down prices and profit margins. Only those with economies of scale and/or sought-after products prosper |
| Within-country transport costs increase somewhat due to the imposition of essential environmental taxes by the government | Dimension B:<br>**Impact of climate change** | The cost of importing products and food from overseas increases dramatically due to increased international transport costs resulting from world wide environmental taxes |

**Figure 7.2** The two scenario dimensions

Today                                                                                        2025

| | | | |
|---|---|---|---|
| Internet shopping is increasingly popular but still not dominant.<br><br>Most people still like to "go shopping".<br><br>People who live in cities and towns can access high-street shops easily.<br><br>Transport costs are getting higher, but are not unreasonable. | People, especially older people with families, move away from city centers as improved technology means they can work from home and move to live where their standard of living is better.<br><br>Cost of transport goes up somewhat due to perceived problems with natural environment – taxes imposed on "unnecessary" travel.<br><br>Competition increases in Internet commerce – pushing down prices. | E-commerce becomes vastly more popular/common.<br><br>Large retailers begin to dominate due to economies of scale. Small, specialist retailers also do well – both through being specialist and by locating locally.<br><br>High-street shopping becomes less popular.<br><br>Costs of stock delivery for retailers increase so that success is aided by scale of operations. | Internet shopping gradually becomes the dominant sales channel.<br><br>Due to the costs of transport, only those general retailers with economies of scale prosper.<br><br>Locally based specialist retailers are only partially affected by the increase in Internet shopping. |

**Figure 7.3** A1B1: The slow, but irresistible, domination of Internet retailing

| | | | |
|---|---|---|---|
| Internet shopping is increasingly popular but still not dominant.<br><br>Most people still like to "go shopping".<br><br>People prefer to choose from a wide range of goods but retailers' attempts to import products from overseas are hampered by increased international transport costs. | People, especially older people with families, move away from city centres as improved technology means they can work from home and move to live where their standard of living is better.<br><br>Competition increases in Internet commerce – driving down prices.<br><br>Strong sensitivity to global warming and its effects, and the occurrence of several natural disasters mean that many governments take action, forced to impose restrictions and taxes on international travel and transportation of food and products across the globe. | Internet shopping becomes vastly more popular/common.<br><br>But providing a broad range of goods to customers becomes more difficult for all retailers.<br><br>Only the global retailers, or specialists, can provide overseas-sourced products.<br><br>Most of the national retailers turn to locally-sourced suppliers, giving these a great deal of power over pricing. | Internet shopping dominates all sales channels. Customers collect Internet purchases from nearby-located depots.<br><br>Since most food and products are nationally sourced, only those retailers with good supplier relations will survive.<br><br>Only those large retailers with economies of scale prosper. Specialist retailers can still provide overseas-sourced goods. |

**Figure 7.4** A1B2: Internet shopping for nationally sourced products and food

| | | | |
|---|---|---|---|
| Internet shopping is commonplace and increasingly a frequent means of purchasing.<br><br>There is a good deal of competition on prices but the costs of delivery are relatively low.<br><br>There is a growing range of Internet retailers who are vying for sales.<br><br>Competition on price is becoming strong.<br><br>Transportation costs increase but are not unreasonable. | There is a strong uptake in Internet shopping as people move away from city centres to live in places where the standard of living is better – improved technology means they can work from home.<br><br>The large retailers increase the level of competition nationally, taking advantage of economies of scale to drive down prices.<br><br>Perceived problems with national natural environment – some taxes levied on travel and transportation | Those large retailers with economies of scale thrive but those without struggle.<br><br>Some consolidation of the market – many smaller retailers go out of business.<br><br>Move towards a model of direct deliveries of a range of good and retail products to each customer by a single multi-retailer. | Due to increased transport costs and price competition, only the big retailers are able to thrive.<br><br>The number of Internet retailers becomes smaller.<br><br>The small specialist high-street shops survive. |

**Figure 7.5** A2B1: The early domination of Internet retailing

**Today**                                                                              **2025**

| | | | |
|---|---|---|---|
| People prefer to choose from a wide range of goods but retailers' attempts to import products from overseas are hampered by increased international transport costs.<br><br>Internet shopping is commonplace and increasingly a frequent means of purchasing. | People, especially older people with families, move away from city centers as improved technology means they can work from home and move to live where their standard of living is better.<br><br>Strong sensitivity to global warming and its effects, and the occurrence of several natural disasters mean that many governments take action, forced to impose restrictions and taxes on international travel and transportation of food and products across the globe. | Only the global retailers, or specialists, can provide overseas-sourced products.<br><br>Most of the national retails turn to locally sourced suppliers, giving these a great deal of power over pricing.<br><br>Those large retailers with economies of scale thrive but those without struggle.<br><br>Some consolidation of the market – many smaller retailers go out of business. | Internet shopping dominates all sales channels. Customers collect Internet purchases from nearby-located depots.<br><br>Only those large retailers with economies of scale prosper. Specialist retailers can still provide overseas-sourced goods.<br><br>The number of Internet retailers becomes smaller.<br><br>The small specialist high-street shops survive. |

**Figure 7.6** A2B2: The domination of a few Internet retailers who are focused on selling nationally sourced products and food

in the A1/B1 scenario, focused on the slow, but irresistible, domination of Internet retailing, it would remain unaffected in the medium-term. Possible strategies for the top-team to consider might include an investigation and evaluation of:

- investment in Internet retailing;
- alliances with a range of organizations already strong in Internet retailing and the underpinning logistic support;
- alliances with a range of organizations that are already strong in the sourcing and transportation of food and products across the world; and
- alliances with a range of door-to-door delivery companies.

But would the alternative strategies endow the high-street retailer with strategic defense against other changes in the business environment that were not captured in the scenario storylines? And which, if any, of the alternative strategies would endow the retailer with strategic opportunism? Our present discussion advocates an additional step, whereby the new strategies should also be evaluated in terms of strategic defense and strategic opportunism. In our view, in this case, the essence of a defensive and opportunistic stance is for the retailer to have a close understanding of:

- changes in what customers want and value, in terms of both products and service levels;
- changes in the locations of where high-quality foods and products are produced; and
- changes in the efficiency and effectiveness of how the foods and products are transported, and so on.

Essentially, the high-street retailer should be sensitive to change in the components in the business environment that might impact the viability of the retailer's current business idea. It follows that the retailer should have some degree of co-involvement with all elements of the value chain that impact on the purchasing behavior of the retailer's customer base. Close relationships with firms that supply products and services to the retailer will allow the retailer to gain early insights into change that will impact the partner firms and, indirectly, the retailer. The retailer should also take an experimental approach to the offering of some new products and services in some of the geographical regions where it operates. In this way, the retailer will ensure that new options are always being tested and evaluated, by encouraging flatness within decision-making. The organization should also avoid harboring a blame culture: experiments with new products and service offerings are risky, and a poor outcome is simply evidence of an attempt to try something new. The retailer's existing partnerships and alliances should be well-rewarded, but contracts and agreements should always be made for the short-term, since existing partnerships and alliances may not be beneficial as the business environment changes. Short-term commitments encourage flexibility in decision-making.

Larger-scale strategic decisions should also be flexible and not be restricted by large prior investments in property and infrastructure. The value of having an option to defer a decision has value. For example, in 1997, Merck signed an agreement with Biogen for Biogen to develop an asthma drug. The agreement involved the scheduled payment of "stage payments" over several years, during which the actual success of the drug's development by Biogen, the state of the drug market, safety rules, and so on, could all change. The stage payments allowed Merck to retain the option, at each stage, either to "scale up" or to "abandon" further involvement in the drug's development. Thus, Merck's upside was unlimited and its downside was capped by the advance payment made to Biogen. In short, there is value in paying for an asset later and earning interest on the money in the meantime,whilst retaining freedom of action. If conditions for an investment improve, then the organization will not lose out. If conditions worsen, then the organization can decide not to acquire an asset and to relinquish the option to do so.

Cornelius *et al.* (2005) give the example of an oil and gas company that had discovered large amounts of natural gas underground in West Africa. However, bringing the natural gas to Europe or North America would require liquefying the gas and transporting it via shipping, a significant additional cost. In the early 1990s, the retail price that could be charged for gas (lower than current prices) meant such a procedure was not viable. However, since that time the natural gas price in both the US and Europe has more than doubled, and the option is now a valuable asset to the company.

Given that some high-impact events may not be included in the scenario storylines, Wright and Goodwin (2009) have also argued that decision-makers should be alert to the degree to which a strategic option is:

- *flexible* – that is, investment can be scaled up or down at any point in the future;
- *diversified* – that is, following the option that diversifies the firm's current major offering(s) by providing a different technology base, or a different production base, or a different customer base;and
- *insurable* – that is, allowing the possibility of insuring against extreme downside risk.

This prescription can be implemented as a necessary checklist that must be completed in any option evaluation, or as part of a more formalized multi-attribute evaluation of options against scenarios – much like the process that we described in Chapter 6.

## SUMMARY

This chapter considered our psychological preparedness for the unexpected. We tend to feel that our judgment is valid and that we are able to predict the future, even though the evidence shows that this is not the case. The hindsight bias is a strong and unconscious way in which we deceive ourselves about our ability to predict the future. The confirmation bias also acts to give us inappropriate confidence in our predictive abilities. Only when high-impact unexpected events occur are our psychological defenses overcome and the sheer unpredictability of the future put into sharp perspective. Scenario thinking, using the conventional intuitive logics method, as we have developed and documented it so far, cannot help us in planning for high-impact rare events. One recourse is to create strategies that provide a defense against inhospitable futures and provide opportunities in the face of favorable futures, as we have discussed in this chapter. As an alternative approach, in Chapter 8 we demonstrate how scenario planning using backwards logic can produce an extended range of scenarios that are more extreme than those produced by the standard intuitive logics methodology. Such broadened scenario thinking can provide decision-makers with insight into the causal unfolding of extreme futures.

# The Backwards Logic Method of Constructing Extreme Scenarios

Until now, our focus in this book has been on using the intuitive logics method of scenario construction as the sole way of constructing our set of scenarios. Recall that the steps include brainstorming the generation of critical uncertainties and predetermined driving forces that will have varying degrees of impact on the focal issue – often, the viability of the organization itself. Recall, also, that the two scenario dimensions are selected from those cluster headings that are judged by scenario team members to be situated in the high-impact low-predictability quadrant of the impact/uncertainty matrix. In earlier chapters, we have demonstrated how each of the relatively independent, high-impact/high-uncertainty clusters is resolved into one of two plausible sets of outcomes: A1 and A2, and B1 and B2. In earlier chapters, we also advocated that each of the two resolutions within a cluster should, in simple terms, be either negative or positive. But does this step-by-step process produce a sufficiently wide range of plausibility in the subsequent four scenarios? Recall our discussion of the retail bank case in Chapter 3. Here, the context of ever-increasing residential housing prices meant that the bank's 2007 scenario thinking workshop did not consider the possibility of the housing market crash in the USA and, later, in many parts of Europe. Can scenario method be adapted to aid the anticipation of high-impact rare events such as this?

Our standard approach first requires that the scenario team members identify predetermined elements and critical uncertainties. These elements are then categorized under the PESTEL headings, next "cross-disciplinary" clusters are constructed between elements, such that causal impacts of one element on another are identified by arrows of influence. In this way, causally linked clusters of driving forces are generated and named that are, to a large degree, independent of one another. The next step is to identify those cluster headings whose content is:

- of high impact on the focal issue of concern (usually the viability of the host or focal organization); and
- of high uncertainty.

The two cluster headings that combine the greatest impact and uncertainty over that the nature of the impact are selected as the scenario dimensions utilized to produce four detailed scenarios – developed with a common, temporal, starting point, but ending in the four diverse, yet plausible, causally-unfolded end-states.

Note that, in general, the two clusters that result from the application of the intuitive logics approach to scenario construction will each contain a mix of pre-determined elements and what are perceived as *critical* uncertainties that are causally linked. Generally, four scenarios are constructed that are derived from the resolution of events within each cluster into two major outcomes, with each of the outcomes of the first cluster then being combined with each of the outcomes of the second cluster. Thus, the resolution of the contents of the two high-impact/high-uncertainty clusters drives the development of the storylines of the four resultant scenarios. The development of the four storylines will, in practice, also utilize other uncertainties and pre-determined elements that have been generated by scenario workshop participants, but which are seen by these participants to have less impact on the focal issue of concern. It follows that each of the four resultant scenarios will be separable from the other three, and also more extreme than the other three in some ways. Since each scenario represents an intersection of resolved uncertainties, each detailed scenario will, logically, have an infinitesimal likelihood of actual occurrence. It also follows that the interactions of resolved uncertainties that are identified by participants, but which are not part of the two high-impact clusters, may have led to the development of quite different scenarios, if they were, instead, taken as the focal uncertainties that drive the construction of the scenarios.

Also, note that the events are linked together in a particular causal chain – where the occurrence of one event causes the occurrence of a subsequent event. For example, consider the components of the chain in Example 8.1.

---

**Example 8.1**

An increase in global warming is perceived to push legal changes that increase carbon-based energy-source taxes for consumers. This, in turn, reduces the use of carbon-based energy, and increases academic and industry-based research into alternative, less-dirty energy sources. Such alternative energy sources are then developed and, later, mass-produced by industry, such that energy use by consumers, after a sharp down-turn immediately following the introduction of carbon taxes, subsequently returns to usage levels just below those prior to the introduction of the tax.

---

Psychologically, this intersection of events – global warming, carbon taxes, lower usage of carbon fuels, successful research into alternatives, and consumer demand for energy not diminishing – will be viewed as a sequence of events whose occurrence is seen as more likely than is logically the case by application of the probability laws. To see this, consider the likelihood of throwing a dice and finding a "six" appearing face-up on six successive throws. The probability of such a string of sixes is 0.00002 – or, in other words, one chance in 50,000. Whilst, in our energy source example, the joint probability of all the events in the causal chain occurring will not be as low as one in 50,000, research has shown that we will tend to think that the joint occurrence of all the events in the causal sequence occurring is higher than it logically should be. As another example, consider which of the situations (adapted from Goodwin and Wright, 2009) in Example 8.2 is the most likely to occur.

---

**Example 8.2**

(a) A decline in the share of the global market of the US computer manufacturing industry during the third decade of the twenty-first century.

(b) A decline in the share of the global market of the US computer manufacturing industry during the third decade of the twenty-first century, as a result of competition from Asian countries such as Japan, Malaysia, South Korea, and China.

---

Most people, when answering this question, indicate that (b) is more likely than (a). But recognize that (a) contains, implicitly, all possible causes, rather than the single cause made explicit in (b). So, logically, (a) is, in fact, more likely to occur than (b).

Thus, having individuals, or groups of individuals, imagining the occurrence of a sequence of events makes the focal sequence appear more likely to occur than the normative probability computed for the intersection of these individually-evaluated events would imply. Tversky and Kahneman (1983) labeled this as a bias due to the operation of the "simulation heuristic". As such, by itself, the act of constructing scenarios may produce increased, but inappropriate, confidence in the likelihood of occurrence of a single scenario. Fortunately, the use of multiple scenarios provides plausible, but *different*, chains of causality. The construction of four scenarios thus provides one potential way to alleviate over-confidence in the unfolding of a single, focal scenario.

However, Healey and Hodgkinson (2008) noted that the increased plausibility of the four focal scenarios may exacerbate another problematic issue: if the components of a scenario are derived from the current mental models of the decision-makers, then these mental models will be strengthened by the operation of the simulation heuristic. As O'Brien (2004) argued, in practice, scenario participants tend to regularly emphasize economic factors – such as exchange rates, interest rates and the focal country's economic activity – as uncertainties that are subsequently given prominence in the scenarios that participants construct. Also, recent and current media-emphasized concerns (e.g. acts of terrorism) tend to replicate themselves in constructed scenarios through the operation of the availability bias (see Chapter 3). O'Brien labeled these practice-recognized issues as "future myopia". There is nothing within the conventional method of constructing scenarios using the intuitive logics methodology that helps the scenario team engage in a broader look at the nature of the future.

## BROADENING THE SCOPE OF CONSTRUCTED SCENARIOS

One way to focus attention on the plausibility of scenarios that have already been constructed is to use the "frame analysis worksheet", developed by Russo and Schoemaker (1989) as an aid to improving decision-making by reducing possible framing biases. The worksheet essentially asks decision-makers to reflect on any aspects of the decision that were consciously omitted in the consideration process. For example, regarding the purchase of a house, questions in the worksheet might elicit responses that either buying a flat or renting a house or flat on a temporary basis was not considered. Also, older houses that need modernization may not be within the decision-maker's current framework of options. In the context of scenario method, Wright and Goodwin advocate the use of the following questions, derived from the frame analysis worksheet, to provoke reflection in the scenario team:

- What boundaries have we put on the scenarios? What aspects have we left out of consideration?
- Why do we think about this question in the way we do?
- What do the scenarios emphasize?
- What do they minimize?
- Do our competitors or our consumers think about these issues differently from the way that we do?

As we argued in Chapter 3, another method to promote the critique of scenarios that have already been constructed is to have members of the scenario team role-play as critics. Devil's advocacy and dialectical inquiry methods promote the critical evaluation of alternative scenarios. However, a structured approach to the development of scenarios is also possible, and it is to an innovation in this process that we turn next.

## CONSTRUCTING SCENARIOS USING BACKWARDS LOGIC

Wright and Goodwin (2009) have proposed a way of broadening the range of scenarios as yet to be developed, whilst, at the same time, retaining the essential focus on causality within the process of scenario construction. Instead of developing scenarios on the basis of the contents of the two high-impact/low-predictability clusters that are identified on the impact/predictability matrix, the scenario team should, instead, focus on plausible changes to the organization's achievement of its objectives, ranging from under-achievement to over-achievement, or from poor achievement to excellent achievement. We next provide a practical step-by-step means by which to implement Wright and Goodwin's method.

## Step 1

Identify the objectives that the organization wishes to achieve through its activities. For example, for profit-seeking organizations, objectives that may be commonly held might be:

- improved market share;
- improved short-term profitability;
- improved cash-flow;
- improved long-term profitability;
- improved return on investments.

For non-profit-seeking organizations, commonly held objectives might include:

- enhanced public awareness of issues;
- greater access to the political arena;
- long-term commitment to action.

## Step 2

For each objective, imagine the range of extreme, but still plausible, outcomes for the organization. The extremes should be high and low, under- and over-achievement, poor and good performance, and so on.

## Step 3

List the factors that could cause these imagined changes in levels of achievement of the organization's key objectives. For example, an extremely negative cash flow could be caused by public concern over the safety of one of the organization's key products or services that results in a step-change downwards in sales of the product or service. Conversely, an extremely positive cash flow could be caused by public concern about a competitor's product or service. A line of questioning should be enacted that identifies the causal chain that results in the extreme achievement, or non-achievement, of a particular key objective.

## Step 4

Investigate if the achievement and non-achievement of a particular key objective could now, with reconsideration, be plausibly made more extreme than that identified at Step 2. If so, Step 3 should be repeated for the more-extreme achievement of the organization's objectives. If not, the scenario team should be encouraged to write down explicit reasons as to why this is viewed to be the case.

To appreciate the power of this backwards logic approach to scenario development, let us, once again, revisit the retail bank case that we discussed in Chapter 3. Recall that the top team's view of the future for the residential housing market included the implicit predetermined element that the increase in residential housing prices would continue, just as it had done for the preceding 15 years. This unchallenged certainty about the future implied the need for the creation of new mortgage products, such that the capital borrowed could be paid off over the course of several generations of a family. Imagine that one key objective of the bank was to preserve its market share and the absolute amount lent to house buyers. What would cause this amount of lending to reduce dramatically? A collapse in house prices and a subsequent collapse in the confidence of people in the benefits of house purchase? What would cause a collapse in house prices? Our step-by-step method, with its inherent focus on causality, would uncover plausible causal chains that underpin extreme changes in the (non-)achievement of the organization's objectives. In this way, scenarios yet to be developed would be broadened and made more extreme, whilst still retaining the essential plausibility that is a key component of the intuitive logics approach to scenario thinking.

This backwards logic approach has the advantage of focusing participants' attention on the possibility of extreme impacts on an organization's objectives. As we argued earlier, forward causal reasoning – that is part of the standard intuitive logics approach to scenario development – may fail to identify these possible impacts because of the huge potential range of causal chains, only a few of which will be the focus in the scenarios; and the absence of a focus on objectives in the scenario construction process.

Wright and Goodwin (2009) provide a short example of the backwards logic approach to scenario development within which the plausibilities of extreme outcomes are evaluated and tested, such that the resulting scenarios retain plausibility. They discuss an example of a London-based, black-cab taxi firm that is interested in understanding future demand for its services in a particular part of London. One of its over-riding objectives is high short-term profit. Profit is driven by revenue, which is driven by the demand for taxi journeys. Apart from weather conditions and other seasonal effects, the owners of the firm believe that demand is influenced by the efficiency of alternative modes of transportation, including buses and subway trains. Imagine that the firm's owners are particularly concerned with the speed of the subway trains on particular routes, reasoning that the faster or slower the journey times, the smaller or greater the demand for taxi services.

One way forward is for the firm to measure average journey times for particular journeys over days and months, and compute averages and measures of dispersion. Assume that measurements exhibit a normal distribution and remain fairly constant over the months. What are the plausible worst and best outcomes for profitability for the taxi firm over the next few years? What would cause a dramatic, but still plausible, weakening in demand? What would cause a dramatic, but still plausible, strengthening in demand? Focusing on the speed of the subway trains, we can intuitively see that a reduction in a particular journey time from 30 minutes to less than 20 minutes is implausible, assuming that investment in new technology will not be made by London Transport in the next few years. By contrast, it is easy to see that a substantial lengthening of journey times is plausible – for example, if bag searches of passengers are introduced in response to further terrorist activity in London. What could cause an increase in terrorist activity in London?

Questions such as this, when focused on the motivations and capabilities of stakeholder groupings (including terrorists, passengers and the London authorities), will reveal each grouping's likely reaction to changes in the contextual environment, and the self-interested actions of each stakeholder grouping as the events within a particular scenario start to unfold. After a range of plausible scenarios has been constructed, the next step would be for the taxi firm to evaluate its strategic options – for example, its ability to scale up its service provision quickly within the particular scenario that we have just outlined.

The steps of the backwards logic approach to scenario development are still focused on identifying causality, but causality that is established by following the chain backwards from an extreme, but still plausible, outcome to its precursor causation in the present day. Thus, the backwards logic method is in contrast to the standard intuitive logics method of scenario development, where the start and end points of an unfolded scenario lie in the components of the two chosen high-impact/high-uncertainty clusters that were identified in the bottom right-hand quadrant of the impact/predictability matrix. Table 8.1 compares and contrasts the two separate, but related, intuitive logics methods.

Wright and Goodwin discuss alternative methods such as incorporating high-impact surprise events that have no inherent causality – that is, no readily apparent causal links between the occurrence of the surprise event and events in the present day. This way of developing scenarios is similar to the approach adopted in crisis management, where an organization tries to prepare for all possible crises "that threaten the viability of the organization and are characterized by ambiguity of cause, effect, and means of resolution" (Pearson and Clair, 1998). The effect, in our view, of preparing an organization for a range of extreme events that have no causal links to the present is best handled by evaluating the organization's preparedness for strategic defense and strategic opportunism, a topic that that we discussed in depth in Chapter 7.

**Table 8.1** Comparison of standard and backwards logic scenario methods

|  | *Conventional intuitive logics method* | *Backwards logic intuitive logics method* |
| --- | --- | --- |
| Underpinning basis for scenario development | Causality | Causality |
| Starting point for scenario development | Components of the chosen two high-impact, high-uncertainty clusters | The (non-)achievement of an extreme in an organization's key objective |
| Number of scenarios that are developed in detail | Four | One or more |
| Focus on stakeholder behavior/reactions in relation to unfolding scenario events | High | High |

## SUMMARY

This chapter has presented the components of the backwards logic approach to aid the construction of scenarios that are more extreme in emphasis than those that are produced by application of the conventional intuitive logics method of scenario development. Both methods, however, share a common emphasis on uncovering causality, and can be distinguished from the construction of scenarios that include the occurrence of surprise high-impact events.

# Diagnosing Organizational Receptiveness

Until now, we have documented our innovations to the scenario method in a rational, step-by-step way, much like following a recipe in a cook book. A methodology is chosen and then applied in a straightforward way to engage an organization's key decision-makers in thinking deeply about the future. But, in reality, organizational life is more complex; a scenario-based intervention that seems, on the face of it, to be uncontroversial and straightforward may not be so.

Consider a large ocean liner that is sinking and likely to submerge over the next few hours. Imagine that you are a passenger on the liner. You look over the side of the ship and notice the heavy rolling waves. The liner's lifeboats are being lowered and you are asked if you want to take a place in a lifeboat. But you consider both the size of the small lifeboats and the size of the waves. Staying on the liner seems risky, but you know that other ships are likely to be in the vicinity and there is talk of a ship-to-ship transfer of the liner's passengers. Should you stay on the sinking liner or claim your place in one of the lifeboats being lowered into the sea? The two options are in conflict, each having advantages and disadvantages. In such situations, stress levels rise. If the time pressure to make a decision is high, both options are risky and no other, safer, options are available, then we tend to *panic* – our stress level continues to rise. If there is less time pressure and more time to think, then we tend to find ways to relieve the stress. We either bolster the current status quo option – for example, by reassuring ourselves that another ship will find our ship and allow us to transfer, or by passing the responsibility of the decision to another – for example, by asking the liner's captain to make the decision, or by delaying our own decision in the hope that other, safer, options will become available. Thus, *bolstering*, *buck-passing* and *procrastination* all serve to lower the stress level inherent in a difficult choice between options. In all cases, there is limited search for more information on which to take a decision, and also limited contingency planning for the difficult outcomes that may result from either choice of options.

By contrast, consider being aboard the same sinking liner but with a large rescue ship already alongside: it is a relatively straightforward decision to change from one ship to another. Here, the decision options – staying with the sinking ship or changing ships – are not in conflict with one another. The change of ships option is an un-conflicted option and so you would, without being overly stressed, choose to step aboard the rescue ship.

Management decision-making can also be an emotional experience, rather than a coolly rational process. We will demonstrate this shortly. For the moment, we will turn our description of decision-making on the sinking liner into a more general, and much more academic, description of the decision processes involved. The formal name for the processes that we have just described is Janis and Mann's (1977) Conflict Theory of Decision-Making, which provides a comprehensive account of decision processes in response to decision dilemmas. Intense conflicts are likely to arise whenever an individual has to make an important decision. Such conflicts become acute as the decision-maker becomes aware of the risk of suffering serious losses from whatever course of action is selected. Decisional conflicts in this context refer to simultaneous opposing tendencies within the individual to accept or reject a given course of action. The most prominent symptoms of such conflicts are hesitation, vacillation, feelings of uncertainty and signs of acute emotional stress whenever a decision comes within the focus of attention.

According to Janis and Mann, several types of decisional behavior called "coping patterns" are the direct result of the conflict: vigilance, hypervigilance, defensive avoidance, unconflicted adherence and unconflicted change .

*Vigilance* is the only coping pattern that results in the careful search for and use of information in the face of a challenge. A precondition for vigilance is that the decision-makers must have concluded that, amongst other things, a better solution to the decision dilemma does exist and that there is adequate time to debate and search for one, the result of which is a moderate level of stress. A vigilant decision would thus not be possible in the sinking ship vignette that we just described.

*Hypervigilance, or panic,* results when the decision-maker is aware that a better solution probably does exist, but perceives that she/he has insufficient time to engage in a search for it.

*Defensive avoidance* arises when the perception is that no better solution exists other than the current course of action, and can take one of three forms:

- *procrastination* – which involves postponing the decision;
- *buck passing* – which involves shifting the responsibility of the decision to someone else; and
- *bolstering* – which includes exaggerating the favorable consequences of the current course of action and minimizing the unfavorable consequences.

Both *hypervigilance* and *defensive avoidance* are preceded by high stress, since there is recognition that the risks associated with adhering to the current option(s) are serious.

*Unconflicted adherence* is preceded by low stress since, here, the decision-maker views the current course of action as unthreatened and the outcomes associated with alternative courses of action as inconsequential. The search for information regarding the consequences of changing a decision is minimal and, since no risks are thought to be associated with it, the current course of action is adhered to. Unconflicted adherence to a decision to stay on the sinking liner in the earlier vignette would thus, also, not be possible.

*Unconflicted change* is also preceded by low stress since, here, a threatened current course of action can be replaced by an alternative, unthreatened course of action. Recall that in our sinking ship vignette this coping pattern was illustrated in the decision to step onto the large rescue ship that was alongside the sinking liner. Figure 9.1 details the essential elements of this theoretical model, as related to the current context of strategic decision-making.

As we shall see in the next section of this chapter, conflict theory can be very useful in diagnosing the organization's receptiveness to a scenario intervention. In order to apply the theory, we need to have information about the thinking of the scenario team who will be involved as members of the scenario workshop. We will show how this can be achieved by interviewing the team members individually and recording their answers to some relatively innocuous questions.

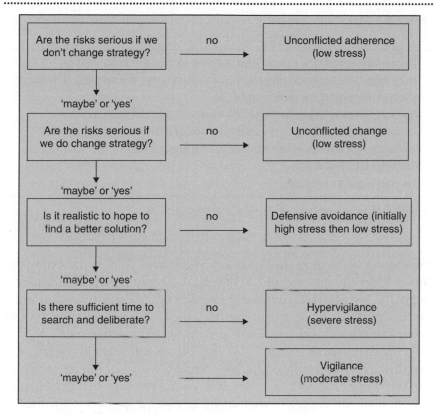

**Figure 9.1** Janis and Mann's Conflict Theory of Decision-Making

## INTERVIEWING MEMBERS OF THE TOP TEAM

Our favored approach to initiating a scenario intervention is to start the process with a number of private interviews with the scenario project team members. The interviews are intended to capture horizons of thinking by allowing each member of the team to voice their views in private and with a guarantee of anonymity. The anonymous nature of the interviews is an important factor, since it allows issues that may not be raised in public to be surfaced to the facilitator. These elicited views express how each member of the team sees the company moving forward and how it will interact with the future competitive environment.

The "trigger" questions that are used to elicit information from those interviewed are given in Table 9.1. These are known, in the scenario literature, as the "7 Questions". They are generalized

**Table 9.1** The seven "trigger" questions used to elicit information from the participants prior to the group meetings

| |
|---|
| 1  The participant's background and current role in the organization |
| 2  Three key issues confronting the organization over the coming decade on which information is much sought |
| 3  Developments relating to these issues under a good scenario |
| 4  Developments relating to these issues under a bad scenario |
| 5  Key/landmark events in the history of the organization |
| 6  Major decisions ahead |
| 7  The participant's epitaph |

Source: Adapted from van der Heijden (1996): 145–9.

questions concerning the future, present and past of the organization, within the context of the external environment. In Chapter 2 (page 29), we utilized a similarly focused set of questions that are a current part of our scenario methodology. The confidential nature of the interviews and resultant anonymity encourage candor.

The outcome of the analysis of the formal interview transcripts is a written report circulated to the scenario team. In our experience, the interview transcripts often result in over one hundred pages of text, and the report is written by grouping quotations from the interviewees on particular issues and concerns where a variety of viewpoints exists. Sample headings for the groupings might include, for example:

- Organization (including sub-groupings of "corporate structure", "people", "leadership", and "morale");
- Politics (including within the focal organization, country and worldwide);
- Operations (including the manufacturing facility, efficiency, production versus R&D, customer-facing activities, and supply-chain);
- Strategic (including in-the-past, here-and-now, expansion, and the future);
- Stakeholders;
- Technology;
- Economics;
- Environment;
- Marketing;
- Decisions.

When a scenario project is not conducted for a single organization but, say, for a community, the viable groupings would, of course, be different. Statements made by individuals are made anonymously and then placed in what, intuitively, seems to be the most appropriate category. The readers of the report are thus in a position to see the degree of convergence – or divergence – of the views of the interviewees on a particular issue or concept. A sample page is shown in Figure 9.2.

---

**Leadership**

"Modern companies need approachable leaders"

"Leaders need to be in touch with the grass roots organization otherwise they make their deasisions in isclation which causes many problems"

"If there were no problems there wouldn't be a need to employ people with big salaries to fix them"

"I think we need belief in ourselves as an organization, not just as a person but with management believing in the person"

"Building bridges across the gaps in the business in a challenge. It requires upper management to take the lead"

"We are lacking the management to do it and the management focus to find out what we need to do for the future"

"The coordination or management of people that's what we are lacking"

**Morale**

"Morale has been hit during the last six months with continual customer pressure to ship etc"

"We don't have a buzz and unless you have a buzz, you may survive but you ultimately will not be hugely successful"

"A lot of people are de-motivated they need to be recharged"

"The organization can benefit tremendously from getting some good successes"

"When a business oxpands and grows people suddenly find their freedom diminishes, the is a danger"

"Attributes we have today may be buried due to disappointment or de-motivation but they are still there"

*Political*

"There are a range of government issues such as, tax, export controls, health and safety legislation that can influence our future"

"Politics are very stable hence this doesn't tend to disrupt us"

"Our government's policy on energy consumption, energy availability and therefore the price of energy is a concern"

---

**Figure 9.2** A sample page from an interview report produced by the authors

The interview transcripts can *also* be organized by the components of Janis and Mann's model in order to enable the scenario facilitator to diagnose the emotional context within the organization that is present at the time of the scenario intervention. Such a diagnosis is, as we will see, useful to the scenario facilitator in enabling evaluation of the organizational receptiveness to the subsequent scenario intervention.

## USING JANIS AND MANN'S THEORY TO ANALYZE THE INTERVIEW MATERIAL

In order to facilitate analysis and interpretation of the interview transcripts, we recommend use of an *a priori* scheme comprising 14 categories that, collectively, embrace the full range of concepts employed within the Janis and Mann Conflict Theory of Decision-Making. An additional miscellaneous category is added to the coding scheme to allow for the possibility that none of the categories derived from this theory were applicable. The coding scheme is presented in full in Table 9.2.

Initially, we recommend that the scenario facilitators read through the set of original interview transcripts and highlight interviewee responses or "quotations" that are, plausibly, illustrations of the various aspects of Janis and Mann's theory. The highlighted responses are then allocated to one of the 14+1 *a priori* categories as considered appropriate, any disagreement between the facilitators as to category allocation being resolved through discussion.

## EXAMPLES OF SCENARIO PRACTICE

We next illustrate our approach, and its benefits, with material from two case studies of our scenario practice.

### Case study 1

The first example of our use of the conflict model to evaluate the emotional context is in a study by Hodgkinson and Wright (2002), which presented data from the interviews of nine individuals comprising the senior management team of a major corporation (Beta Co) facing a crucial strategic decision dilemma. The interviews

**Table 9.2** The coding schedule used to re-analyze the pre-workshop interview transcripts

| *Category no.* | *Description* |
|---|---|
| 1 | The individual believes the risks *are* serious if the organization *keeps* to its current strategy |
| 2 | The individual believes the risks *are* serious if the organization *changes* its current strategy |
| 3 | The individual believes the risks are *not* serious if the organization *keeps* to its current strategy |
| 4 | The individual believes the risks are *not* serious if the organization *changes* its current strategy |
| 5 | The individual believes there is *insufficient* time to search for (and fully consider) a new strategy to *replace* the current strategy |
| 6 | The individual believes there is *sufficient* time to search for (and fully consider) a new strategy to *replace* the current strategy |
| 7 | The individual believes that it is *realistic* to hope to find a better strategy to *replace* the one currently being followed |
| 8 | The individual believes that it is *unrealistic* to hope to find a better strategy to *replace* the one currently being followed |
| 9 | The individual (or wider organization) is *delaying* (or putting off) making a strategic choice |
| 10 | The individual (or wider organization) is *shifting the responsibility* for making a strategic choice to another individual or group of individuals |
| 11 | The individual (or wider organization) is engaged in *exaggerating the positive* consequence (or minimizing the negative consequence) of the *current* strategy |
| 12 | The quotation indicates either:<br>– *limited evaluation* of available information; or<br>– *limited planning* for events that could happen |
| 13 | The quotation indicates high-quality strategic decision-making |
| 14 | The quotation indicates *panic* |
| 15 | The quotation *does not fit* any of the other categories |

were conducted prior to a scenario construction exercise in which all of the interviewees were subsequently active participants. There was clear evidence that the organization's current strategic direction was failing, and that the management team were experiencing difficulty in developing acceptable, alternative strategies. Although it was apparent that Beta Co. had strong competencies underpinning its existing business idea, it was equally apparent that there was no longer alignment between this idea and the requirements of a changing environment. Quotations from the management team interview data collected were categorized under Janis and Mann's headings.

The following exemplar comments illustrate that the management team perceived the risks to be serious, if the organization failed to change its current strategy:

*Participant 1*: The business needs more income streams ... therefore, diversification is crucial now to build significant other income streams.

*Participant 2*: A key danger is that there is too much emphasis on our core business activity ... New technology could result in the death of [Beta Co's main offering] by 2005, 2010, 2015. Who knows when? We need to move to new areas that will result in new revenue streams ... The failure of [Beta Co] to develop alternative revenue streams would be another bad scenario.

*Participant 3*: If we go on as we are, in 10 years from now we won't be here.

*Participant 5*: There is a perception around here that [Beta Co] has very much got all its eggs together in one basket. If one of [Beta Co's major customers] pulled out ... At a personal level, I am very much concerned that we have job security.

At the same time, the risks were also perceived to be serious if the organization did change its strategy, as is illustrated by the following quotations:

*Participant 4*: We are a group of talented amateurs rather than experienced in areas of potential diversification.

*Participant 6*: [Beta's latest experimental venture] has been a protracted and salutary experience. There are very few short-term gains to be made.

*Participant 7*: We are naïve on the business side [Beta Co's latest experiment venture] is necessary for our future, but we have had a slightly unrealistic view of how easy or difficult it would be to break into an existing market in which potential customers have settled relationships and [Beta Co] has no track record.

It was also clear, as evidenced from the quotations that follow, that the senior management team was also attempting to shift responsibility (i.e. "pass the buck") to the board of directors of the company for adhering to a strategy that was obviously failing:

*Participant 1*: Our main board director is on the record as having said that [Beta Co] should make an attempt to adapt to changing market conditions.

*Participant 3*: The board faces a key decision, not us. They need to take a keen interest in terms of what shape [Beta Co] should take in the future.

*Participant 7*: We have to try and resolve the diversification issue one way or the other, but I am not sure that this is a decision we can take.

Equally, there was also compelling evidence of delay and procrastination amongst the management team, as demonstrated by the following comments:

*Participant 1*: The failure to diversify would probably mean the business would still be OK in 10 years from now, but after 15 years it would be starting to decline.

*Participant 5*: There is still mileage in [Beta Co's offering] for the next 10 years.

*Participant 6*: Things will be slower than most people think ... We are 20 years away from complete change i.e. our business will still be serviceable in 20 years' time.

*Participant 7*: There is no real rush to adapt ... five to 10 years away there will still be a healthy market for [Beta Co's main offering].

Finally, there was evidence of bolstering the current failing strategy:

> *Participant 2*: The slow part of change in our industry is of bene-fit to us … if [Beta Co] becomes the only [provider of its current main offering] there will be less pressure on us to develop other products … [Beta Co's] current performance and historic record are its key strength.

> *Participant 2*: One of the problems we face in respect of new product is customer inertia … Customers are generally conserva-tive because they don't want the hassle of changing [suppliers]. These same forces are potentially prolonging the life of [Beta Co's current main offering] … within the next two to three years.

> *Participant 2*: Ultimately, I was brought in [to Beta Co] to play a key role in enabling the organization to diversify and/or add to its core business, though diversification may not be needed if [Beta Co.] becomes [the major player within the market of its current main offering] within the next two to three years.

To summarize to this point: the company's strategy was failing and the management team was having difficulty developing a new strategy; members were aware that failure to change the strat-egy – that is, "do nothing" – was a high risk option but, equally, perceived risks in making changes; and evidence of all three defensive avoidance behaviors (buck passing, procrastination and bolstering) were present.

At the same time, the following comments indicate that there was also clearly a deficiency in terms of information search and contingency planning.

> *Participant 1*: I believe you can always buy the skill you need. You may have to pay a bit more or wait a bit.

> *Participant 4*: We don't know enough about the real strategic aims of [Beta Co's main customers].

> *Participant 4*: We lack understanding of real customer require-ments … We know even less about potential customers.

*Participant 5*: There is a learning process we need to go through, but I am sure we can do it and beat the competition.

*Participant 2*: Another key requirement is for investment in R&D to secure the organization's future through the creation of new revenue streams, but how should this be done?

*Participant 5*: I guess we ought to be doing other things to protect ourselves.

Hodgkinson and Wright concluded that the subsequent scenario construction exercise put the nature of the future into sharp focus for Beta Co. It revealed that several technological changes, regarded by the participants as predetermined factors rather than critical uncertainties, would eventually replace the company's main offering. Unfortunately, none of the strategic alternatives devised by the participants was robust against the range of futures constructed in the scenarios and, essentially, the company could only continue with its current strategy. Consequently, this scenario exercise was considered an unsuccessful intervention. According to the Janis and Mann model, if an appropriate alternative strategy cannot be devised, unconflicted change is not possible; in such a situation the pre-intervention stress level is raised again to an unacceptable level and, once more, a range of psychological defense mechanisms come into effect, ultimately inhibiting the change management process itself. This is what happened in the Beta Co case: the scenario process served only to "rub salt into a wound" that had been superficially healed by the earlier enactment of psychological coping processes.

## Case study 2

In January 2005, Alpha-A, a wholly owned subsidiary of Alpha, had established itself as a major player in the specialized engine management unit business. An engine management unit is an electronic component that monitors and adjusts engine systems to cope efficiently and effectively with varied operating environments. As a consequence of sustained economic growth, especially in Asia, sales of engine management units were growing at 10 percent (compound annual average growth rate) and the existing manufacturing capacity at Alpha-A was deemed unlikely to meet the demands of the future.

Following a review of the specialized-engine industry and market worldwide, of which engine management units were a major part, Alpha embarked upon a plan to raise in excess of US$34 million to expand the production capacity to approximately 100,000 units a year from the existing capacity of approximately 20,000 units per year. This investment represented the largest single investment in the company's 30-year history.

In May 2005, having failed to raise the necessary funds for the expansion of production from conventional sources of investment, the board took the decision to sell the most profitable division of Alpha (Alpha-B) for approximately US$250 million. The raised cash would result in a return to the shareholders, the elimination of debt, and funds for the expansion.

In June 2005, a reappraisal of the assumptions and data used to justify the fivefold expansion suggested that a more modest expansion might be appropriate. As a consequence of these uncertainties, the company decided to re-evaluate its position, with three levels of expansion proposed: 55,000 units per year, 75,000 units per year and 100,000 units per year, over a three-year period. In repositioning the levels of the expansion and the necessary funds to achieve each target production run, the decision to sell Alpha-B was brought into question.

In August 2005, the scenario intervention took place with Alpha-A's top team in order to re-visit the decision to expand capacity. We now summarize the interview-based findings of O'Keefe and Wright (2010) and, again, use the Janis and Mann categories to evaluate the yield of the pre-scenario intervention interviews that were conducted with the senior management team members.

Would Alpha-A be at serious risk if it didn't change its current strategy? Five of the interviewed participants presented a view that the short-term strategy being operated – that is, the decision, in principle, to expand production in line with the major customer's view of its future needs – was damaging the long-term future of the company, as illustrated by the following remark:

*Director 1*: I don't think we are doing much significant research and I think that even within five years the company is jeopardized by that short-term view.

Only the Chief Executive Officer did not vocalize that the expansion of manufacturing production was risky. Illustrations of the comments of the other directors were:

> *Director 2*: We are placing an over reliance on one customer ... we haven't got the protection of a sound commercial agreement with that customer that would (a) allow us to sleep at night, and (b) can justify the investment we are just about to make.

> *Director 2*: If you stand back and look at the organization as a high volume, low margin, all year, unbranded, unknown entity, it's not exactly a great business model (FD)

> *Director 3*: I think there is tunnel vision on where we should be going. I think there is a serious lack of strategy. I think we are getting very, very, hung up with one customer who actually is quite untrustworthy as a customer.

> *Director 4*: I think we're poor on [manufacturing].

> *Director 2*: So we could have a little bit of egg on our faces were we to ramp up to 55k volume ... and then suddenly it isn't required.

Would the risks to Alpha-A be serious if it does change its current strategy? The organization was dependent on one customer – as is illustrated in the following comment:

> *Director 2*: At the moment we are a one trick pony

This situation seems to be further exacerbated by the fact that most directors didn't believe all the business activities were up to scratch, consequently making a change in the business model (away from volume manufacturing) difficult and risky:

> *Director 2*: At this moment in time we are a relatively small player in some markets, the merchant market, to a certain extent the defense market and we never got into [a new business area] properly – we probably missed the boat there. It's how quickly we

can develop other business areas in the next three to five years that will again determine our future.

*Director 3*: We're very, very, one opportunity at the moment and even new opportunities that we could have, that gives us our margin, we've either not got [the stuff] ... or the stuff that we have got is wrong.

*Director 5*: We are rather a technology company than a business orientated company. And so, we are lacking, I think, expertise from the business perspective.

*Director 5*: We have good people, we have gaps – we certainly have gaps!

*Chief Executive Officer*: I think we probably still need to do more work in terms of business development and marketing.

Was it realistic to hope to find a better solution for Alpha-A's current strategic dilemma? The answer to this question is not straightforward. On the one hand, some directors believed there was hope but felt more "influential" directors were ignoring their opinions; thus, those who were supportive of an alternative strategy were being marginalized. On the other hand, there was a belief that the major problem was that the operation of the business was running against the "stated" strategy and that the "executed" strategy was damaging the longevity of the company. The *stated* strategy was to use the volume engine management unit manufacturing business (a low-margin product) to maintain the facility/infrastructure (that is, to pay the bills) with priority given to develop new products (with higher margins) and new revenues.

The *executed* strategy was, as noted earlier, to give priority to the major customer whose only interest was in the lower-margin engine management units. The following statement from one Director illustrates this point:

*Director 1*: If the strategy's how I believe it to be then we need to actually follow it because ... at almost every opportunity of decision-making the decisions actually go against the [stated] strategy.

In O'Keefe and Wright's (2010) view, it was obvious that a number of directors felt marginalized, and thus impotent to direct the company on a more sustainable path. The Chief Executive Officer, who was the sole member of Alpha-A to sit on the executive board of Alpha, could not accept alternatives to the "executed" strategy; although there appears to be a realization, by the other directors, that the present state of affairs was unacceptable:

> *Director 2*: So there will be opportunities undoubtedly ... but its our ability to exploit those in the market place for profit, I'd say, is probably our greatest weakness.

> *Director 3*: I wouldn't necessarily say, I would [expand the capacity] as far as where they are now saying they are going to go as well. I would continue to look into new business opportunities.

> *Director 3*: There are a number of opportunities that we could be designing in if any kind of priority was given to that.

> *Director 1*: [The stated] strategy is kind of either being dropped or just being completely ignored.

> *Director 1*: There is a distinct lack of vision in the organization, or where there is vision it's being ignored.

The marginalization of a number of directors provided an excuse to blame others for the position in which the organization found itself. This shifting of responsibility was also evident in those directors who appeared to have maintained their influence. There was frequent use of the word "we", meaning the directors, when it appeared that this should have been "I". Director 4 was quite honest about shifting the blame:

> *Director 4*: I'm not sure I'm going to be much help, other than to ... because I wasn't party to a lot of that. So that was pulled together essentially by [Directors 2 and 3], I'd made input with [the operations manager at the time]'s help in terms of tool cost and things like that. I think what everybody said at the time, and we can blame [the former Chief Executive Officer] for that, because [he's] gone, was that these numbers are just far too big.

There were a number of instances where responsibility for the issues was deflected or deferred to others:

*Director 2*: That's probably a weakness that we don't have certain individuals, class individuals, or indeed the structure.

*Chief Executive Officer*: It's hard for me because I've only been here 18 months.

*Director 1*: I think you have to be very careful who you choose to fill the higher levels of the organization and we've done poorly in that area recently.

*Director 1*: I don't know, I'm rather technically focused.

*Director 4*: A view was taken (not mine).

*Director 4*: Cost us because it's put [the managing director of another division] in a very strong position. His business has probably slowed us down in growing the bespoke business.

*Director 4*: [Director 2 is] a big proponent of hedging ... and the [group finance officer at the time] decided that he wouldn't for whatever reasons.

In some cases, this extended to entities outside the company. On a number of occasions, participants expressed the opinion that the company's best future lay in the hands of another company:

*Director 2*: If, we choose truly to get into bed with [major customer] for the short term, then the best outcome would be for them to buy us for the future of the business.

*Director 1*: If we can't manage our own future somebody else will.

Shifting responsibility is recognized as a defensive avoidance strategy, as is procrastination. There were many references in all interview transcripts to "we have to", or "we need to". The use of the future tense was pervasive in the transcripts:

*Director 2*: It's how quickly we can develop other business areas in the next three to five years that will again determine our future.

*Director 3*: I would continue to look into new business opportunities

*Director 3*: I think the one thing we don't do well is we continue flogging a dead horse for a long time.

*Director 5*: We're operating in flux ... [the company] needs to be stabilized.

*Chief Executive Officer*: I would like to see some changes in the organization going forward.

*Chief Executive Officer*: But where the long-term destiny of the company is going is something that we need to work on

Although there was a general acceptance that elements of the present situation had to change, there seemed a reluctance to do so, as evidenced in the statements illustrating procrastination. At the same time, there was strong bolstering of the current, failing operational strategy:

*Director 2*: I would look at it ... in terms of the [specialized engine] market and our relationship with [major customer]. On the positive side, they look the part and are fully with us.

*Director 3*: I seriously believe we needed that opportunity for us to get into profitability ... I actually think if it wasn't for the [engine management unit] we would be closed by today.

*Chief Executive Officer*: I think this resource, this facility, is just one of our enormous strengths right now. And we actually have to exploit that; quite frankly, we've put a lot of money into it so we now have to exploit it.

*Director 4*: I would argue that if we hadn't got that business then ... I'm not sure this [manufacturing base] would have made it ... it's kept us going and we've got the volume ... but we ain't making a lot of money.

O'Keefe and Wright argued that the directors of Alpha-A exhibited all three of the defensive avoidance strategies postulated by

Janis and Mann. These avoidance strategies had a negative impact on *information search* and *contingency planning*, as illustrated in the following comments:

*Director 3*: I don't think there's enough more volume, higher margin work out there for us to capture to make the [manufacturing base] profitable.

*Chief Executive Officer*: There might be some little lab somewhere which we don't know anything about that pops up with a eureka.

*Chief Executive Officer*: One of the decisions that we have to make is ... where do we actually see the market going.

*Chief Executive Officer*: Understanding the market is something which we are still really trying to do.

*Director 1*: I don't think there's anything, particularly at the moment, that ... is disruptive.

*Director 1*: I certainly think there is a lack of understanding in the markets.

*Director 4*: It was a guesstimate.

*Director 2*: But it could easily flip round ... change in the technology in the [engine management unit] product ... then all of a sudden all of the [current manufacturers] will start twiddling their thumbs.

*Director 3*: Once there ends up being excess capacity, I think that we may be quite exposed.

*Chief Executive Officer*: The biggest risk has to be that somebody just comes up with something which says, we don't need [current technology engine management unit] in 12 or 18 months – that would be a big challenge for us. But, as you know, we don't see that at this time.

*Chief Executive Officer*: There is the general issue of how much money we do set aside for R&D.

*Chief Executive Officer:* If the EU economy took a great turn up or some of the technology parks locally all fired up big time, we could lose quite a lot of people and that could cause a problem.

The above analysis again demonstrates the operation of elements of the defensive avoidance mechanisms predicted by Janis and Mann's conflict theory. O'Keefe and Wright argued that these defensive strategies were engaged as a result of stress induced by an acceptance that the decision on expansion was fraught with risk. The timing of the scenario process intervention could not have been worse. The divestiture of the Alpha-B business was high in the consciences of the directors. The loss of the major part of Alpha's business was going to have a large effect on the form of Alpha-A. As the Chief Executive Officer stated:

*Chief Executive Officer:* A very large part of the business is going to be sold and we will end up with a new shape of company.

## SUMMARY

Our two case analyses illustrate the operation of Janis and Mann's theory within the top teams of two very different organizations. In Case study 1, Beta Co. had been unable to identify an unconflicted change of strategy, and the subsequent scenario planning intervention served to inflame the situation by bringing the impotence of the organization and its leadership into sharp focus.

Shifting responsibility, procrastination and bolstering the currently-failing strategy were evident, as was poor information search and contingency planning. In Case study 2, Alpha-A's top management team were divided in their views of the current strategy. The Chief Executive Officer wanted to follow one direction, whilst the rest of the top management team perceived fundamental weaknesses in that strategic direction. As in Case study 1, all the elements of Janis and Mann's coping patterns were evidenced. Wright *et al.* (2008) have shown, by contrast, that scenario interventions are more straightforward in organizational contexts where the host organization perceives that the risks in changing strategy are not serious – that is, unconflicted change of strategy is seen as possible – and continuing with the current business-as-usual strategy is also seen to be devoid of risk. In such instances, as expected, evidence of the operation of Janis and Mann's coping patterns is slight. In short, scenario interventions are easiest when the host organization is content with its current strategy, but is prepared to consider alternatives. But, of course, such an organizational context is likely to provide no impetus for engaging in a scenario intervention in the first place, since all is seen to be well with the current strategy. Why, then, bother considering alternatives? By our analysis, most scenario interventions are likely to take place in stressful situations – where the risks of continuing with the business-as-usual strategy, or changing strategy, are salient to the top management team. Such situations are, as we have documented in this chapter, potentially problematic for those facilitating the scenario intervention.

What are the implications of our analysis of our two cases for reflective practitioners? Heifetz and Neustadt (1994), psychiatrists, have argued that adaptive work is needed to allow group participants to be open about their individual viewpoints and to facilitate change of opinion in stressful situations – such as the ones we encountered. Successful scenario practitioners need to be able to gauge, cognitively and emotionally, how far to challenge individuals in the process of enabling vigilant decision-making. Clearly, the yield of the pre-intervention interviews deserves close attention by scenario intervention facilitators. Further, application of Janis and Mann's Conflict Theory of Decision-Making demonstrably provides a useful lens with which to analyze the interview material.

# Summary

As we saw in Chapter 1, many organizations do not see the value of scenario analysis: they view the future as an extrapolation of the past, and so continue with business-as-usual. Other organizations do sense that the future holds threats and opportunities, but can become caught in the psychological defense of a failing strategy – by procrastination, bolstering and buck-passing, as we saw in Chapter 9. Scenario thinking can help individuals think more broadly about the nature of the future and, in this book, we have presented a step-by-step approach to scenario thinking that will enable you to implement the intuitive logics scenario method without the aid of an external facilitator. Our approach has been decision-focused, in that the scenarios built by our method are immediately relevant to a focal issue facing an organization.

The conventional scenario method of intuitive logics can be augmented, and several of the chapters in this book have demonstrated the use and power of these augmentations:

- critiquing part-developed scenarios, such that inappropriate framings on the nature of unfolding futures are identified;
- role-playing of stakeholder reactions to the unfolding events within a particular scenario, such that part-developed scenarios achieve greater realism;
- understanding the impact of unfolding futures on the less-powerful but still impacted stakeholders, thus allowing you to reflect on the social desirability of an organization's actions and reactions to an unfolding future;
- providing a structured way of evaluating the performance of options against scenarios using a multi-attributed value approach;
- evaluating strategic options for strategic defense and strategic opportunism in the face of high-impact events of low predictability;
- constructing a range of extreme scenarios that are still causally-linked to the present by backwards logic; and

- diagnosing whether the organizational context is appropriate for a scenario intervention by analyzing the content of pre-intervention interview responses.

The contents of our book have been based, in part, on our academic research and, in part, on the reality-testing of our academic advances in the real-world via our consultancy practice. Thus, our recommended implementation of the intuitive logics scenario method, and our recommended enhancements and augmentations of the method have a grounding that is both strongly academic and practical.

The essence of the intuitive logics approach is causality, and this essential element is preserved throughout our range of enhancements of the basic method. Scenario method is specifically designed as an approach to problem investigation and analysis that is:

- *inclusive* – in that it involves and engages with all relevant stakeholders who are represented in the scenario team;
- *democratic* – in providing an open forum for the expression of all views and opinions; scenario thinking does not respect hierarchy – the best insights can come from any member of the scenario team;
- *non-selective* – in presenting a range of possible and plausible future conditions without making judgments on which is more or less likely to unfold in reality; and
- *possibly threatening* – in that it will challenge both business-as-usual thinking and the individually held perspectives of scenario team members.

We hope that you and your organization(s) are now prepared to face up to the challenges of undertaking scenario analysis in order to gain insights into the future and improved decision-making in the present. We wish you success with your own endeavors in applying scenario thinking.

George Wright and George Cairns can be contacted at
Scenariothinkers@gmail.com

# Appendix

## SUGGESTED TIMETABLE FOR A 24-HOUR SCENARIO PROJECT

If you are undertaking a short, exploratory scenario project, you can consider bringing a group together for one day and undertaking the "basic method", as set out in Chapter 2. However, our experience indicates that a one-day project has limitations, in that participants are required to work intensively throughout the day, and may become tired and less critical as the crucial stages of creative and challenging thinking are undertaken. Also, within an intense, single-day exercise, participants have little or no time to sit back and reflect upon their thinking.

We have found that a 24-hour scenario exercise is much more productive, with fresher minds at the crucial stages, and the chance for informal discussion and group reflection if an overnight stay is required. The following timetable outlines a typical set of timings that we have found appropriate for 24-hour exercises.

Day1: Afternoon (1.00 pm–5.30pm)

| Stage | Arrival and general introductions | | 12:00–13:00 |
|---|---|---|---|
| | Introduction to the Scenario Workshop | | 13:00–13:15 |
| 1 | Setting the Agenda | Defining the issue and process | 13:15–13:45 |
| 2 | Determining the Driving Forces | Working individually, then as a group | 13:45–14.30 |
| 3 | Clustering the Driving Forces | Group discussion to develop, test and name clusters | 14.30–15.10 |
| | | Tea/coffee | 15:10–15:30 |
| 4 | Defining the Cluster Outcomes | Extreme outcomes for each of the clusters over the agreed timescale | 15:30–16:30 |

| 5 | *Impact/Uncertainty Matrix* | Determining the scenario framing factors A and B | 16:30–17.00 |
| | Summary Day 1 | | 17.00–17.15 |
| | | Reception, informal discussion followed by dinner | 17:30 onwards |

**Day2: Morning (9.00 am–1.00pm)**

| *Stage* | *Welcome Back, overview of Day 1 plus overnight insights* | | *09:00–09:15* |
|---|---|---|---|
| 6 | *Framing the Scenarios* | Defining extreme outcomes for the key scenario factors, A and B | 09:15–9.30 |
| 7 | *Scoping the Scenarios* | Building the set of descriptors for 4 scenarios | 09.30–10.00 |
| 7b | *Stakeholder Analysis* | Determining the stakeholders and their place in each scenario | 10.00–10.45 |
| | | Coffee/tea | 10:45–11.05 |
| 8 | *Developing the Scenarios* | Working in sub-groups to develop scenario storylines | 11.05–12:00 |
| | Group summary presentations and questions | | 12:00–12:45 |
| | Session wrap-up and follow-up planning | | 12:45–13:00 |
| | | Lunch and departure | 13.00 |

In implementation, we have been very assertive in ensuring that the times are held to, in order to ensure completion. This example, you will note, includes the optional Stage 7b: *Stakeholder Analysis* (see Chapter 5), in order to provide a "broad" stakeholder consideration to the scenario storylines and how their impact is assessed.

In facilitating a substantial number of such 24-hour scenario projects, we have found on many occasions that participants come to Day 2 having woken at 6.00 am, 5.00 am, or even earlier with some 'Aha!' response to issues that have emerged in Day 1. These insights then contribute to the analysis and scenario development in Day 2, adding depth, clarity, or increased plausibility and credibility to the scenario storylines.

# References

Alfaro, L. and Kim, R. (2009/2010) *U.S. Subprime Mortgage Crisis: Policy Reactions (B)*. Boston, MA: Harvard Business School Publishing.

Beech, N. and Cairns, G. (2001) "Coping with Change: The contribution of postdichotomous ontologies", *Human Relations*, 54(10): 1303–24.

Berger, P.L. and Luckmann, T. (1966) *The Social Construction of Reality: A Treatise in the Sociology of Knowledge*. New York: Anchor Books/ Doubleday.

Bradfield, R., Wright, G., Cairns, G., van der Heijden, K. and Burt, G. (2005) "The Origins and Evolution of Scenario Techniques in Long Range Business Planning", *Futures*, 37: 795–812.

Cairns, G. (2007) "Postcard from Chittagong: Wish you were here?", *Critical Perspectives on International Business*, 3(3): 266–79.

Cairns, G. and Śliwa, M. (2008) *A Very Short, Fairly Interesting and Reasonably Cheap Book About International Business*. London: SAGE.

Cairns, G., Śliwa, M. and Wright, G. (2010) "Problematizing International Business Futures through a 'Critical Scenario Method'", *Futures*, 42: 971–9.

Cairns, G., Wright, G., Bradfield, R., van der Heijden, K. and Burt, G. (2006) "Enhancing Foresight between Multiple Agencies: Issues in the use of scenario thinking to overcome fragmentation", *Futures*, 38: 1011–25.

Cairns, G., Wright, G., van der Heijden, K., Burt, G. and Bradfield, R. (2004) "The Application of Scenario Planning to Internally-Generated e-Government Futures", *Technological Forecasting and Social Change*, 71: 217–38.

Cerf, C. and Nevasky, V (1998) *The Experts Speak: The Definitive Compendium of Authoritative Misinformation*. New York/Toronto: Villard Books/ Random House.

Cornelius, P., Van de Putte, A. and Romani, M. (2005) "Three Decades of Scenario Planning in Shell", *California Management Review*, 48: 92–109.

de Geus, A. (1999) *The Living Company*. London: Nicholas Brealey Publishing.

De Jouvenal, B. (1967) *The Art of Conjecture*. London: Weidenfeld & Nicolson.

Eriksson, E.A. and Weber, K.M. (2008) "Adaptive Foresight: Navigating the complex landscape of policy strategies", *Technological Forecasting and Social Change*, 75: 462–82.

Fischhoff, B. (1975) "Hindsight? Foresight: The effect of outcome knowledge on judgment under uncertainty", *Journal of Experimental Psychology: Human Perception and Performance*, 1: 288–99.

Flyvbjerg, B. (1998) *Rationality and Power: Democracy in practice*. Chicago: University of Chicago Press.

Flyvbjerg, B. (2001) *Making Social Science Matter: Why Social Inquiry Fails and How It Can Succeed Again*. Cambridge: Cambridge University Press.

Flyvbjerg, B. (2003) "Making Organization Research Matter: Power values and phronesis", in B. Czarniawska and G. Sevón (eds), *The Northern Lights: Organization Theory in Scandinavia*. Copenhagen: Liber Abstrakt – Copenhagen Business School Press, 357–82.

Freeman, R.E. (1994) "The Politics of Stakeholder Theory: Some future directions", *Business Ethics Quarterly*, 4(4) 409–21.

Freeman, R.E. and Reed, D.L. (1983) "Stockholders and Stakeholders: A new perspective on corporate governance", *California Management Review*, XXV(3), spring.

Goodwin, P. and Wright, G. (2001) "Enhancing Strategy Evaluation in Scenario Planning: A role for decision analysis", *Journal of Management Studies*, 38, 1–16.

Goodwin, P. and Wright, G. (2009) *Decision Analysis for Management Judgment*, 4th edn. Chichester and New York: John Wiley, September.

Goodwin, P. and Wright, G. (2010) "The Limits of Forecasting Methods in Anticipating Rare Events", *Technological Forecasting and Social Change*, 77: 355–68.

Green, K.C. and Armstrong, J.S. (2011) "Role-thinking: Standing in Other People's Shoes", *International Journal of Forecasting*, 27: 69–80.

Hamel, G. (2000) *Leading the Revolution*. Boston: Harvard Business School Press.

Healey, M.P. and Hodgkinson, G.P. (2008) "Troubling Future: Scenarios and scenario planning for organizational decision making", In G.P. Hodgkinson and W. Starbuck (eds), *Organizational Decision Making*. Oxford: Oxford University Press.

Heifetz, R.A. and Neustadt, R.A. (1994) *Leadership Without Easy Answers*. Cambridge, MA: Harvard University Press.

Hodgkinson, G.P. (2001) "The Psychology of Strategic Management: Diversity and cognition revisited", in C.L. Cooper and I.T. Robertson (eds), *International Review of Industrial and Organizational Psychology*, vol.16, Chichester: Wiley: 65–119.

Hodgkinson, G.P. and Sparrow, P.R. (2002) *The Competent Organization: A Psychological Analysis of the Strategic Management Process*. Buckingham: Open University Press.

Hodgkinson, G.P. and Wright, G. (2002) "Confronting Strategic Inertia in a Top Management Team: Learning from failure, *Organization Studies*, 23: 949–77.

Hughes, N. (2009) "A Historical Overview of Strategic Scenario Planning", Working Paper of the UKERC and EON/EPSRC Transition Pathways Project, UK Energy Research Centre.

Hyde, A.C. (1999) "Scenario Planning: Strategic thinking goes back to the future", *The Public Manager: The New Bureaucrat*, 28(3): 62.

Janis, I.L. and Mann, L. (1977) *Decision-Making: A Psychological Analysis of Conflict*. New York: Free Press.

Jungermann, H. and Thuring, M. (1987) "The Use of Mental Models for Generating Scenarios", in G. Wright and P. Ayton (eds), *Judgmental Forecasting*. London: John Wiley.

Makridakis, S., Hogarth, R.M. and Gaba, A. (2009)" Forecasting and Uncertainty in the Economic and Business World", *International Journal of Forecasting*, 25: 794–812.

Marchau, V.A.W.J., Walker, W.E. and, van Wee, G.P. (2010) "Dynamic Adaptive Transport Policies for Handling Deep Uncertainty", *Technological Forecasting and Social Change*, 77: 940–50.

Maslow, A.H. (1943) "A Theory of Human Motivation", *Psychological Review*, 50: 370–96.

Mintzberg, H. (1994) *The Rise and Fall of Strategic Planning*. New York: Free Press.

Mintzberg, H., Ahlstrand, B. and Lampel, J. (1998) *Strategy Safari: The complete guide through the wilds of strategic management*. London: Prentice Hall.

Nemeth, C., Brown, K. and Rogers, J. (2001) "Devil's Advocate versus Authentic Dissent: Stimulating quantity and quality", *European Journal of Social Psychology*, 31: 707–20.

O'Brien, F.A. (2004) "Scenario Planning: Lessons for practice from teaching and learning", *European Journal of Operational Research*, 152: 709–22.

O'Keefe, M. and Wright, G. (2010) "Non-receptive Organizational Contexts and Scenario Planning Interventions: A demonstration of inertia in the strategic decision making of a CEO, despite strong pressure for change", *Futures*, 42: 26–41.

Pearson, C.M. and Clair, J.A. (1998) "Reframing Crisis Management", *Academy of Management Review*, 23: 59–76.

Pearson, C.M., Clair, J.A., Hisra, S.K. and Mitroff, I.I. (1997) "Managing the Unthinkable", *Organizational Dynamics*, autumn: 51–4.

Porter, M.E. (1985) *Competitive Advantage: Creating and sustaining superior performance*. New York: Free Press.

Rigby, A., and Bilodeau, B. (2007) "A Growing Focus on Preparedness", *Harvard Business Review*, July–August: 21–2.

Roeder, M. (2010) *The Big Mo: Why Momentum Now Rules Our World*. Sydney: HarperCollins.

Russo, J.E. and Schoemaker, P.J.H. (1989) *Confident Decision Making*. London: Piatkus.

Schoemaker, P.J.H. (1993) Multiple scenario development: its conceptual and behavioural foundation, *Strategic Management Journal* 14: 192–213.

Schoemaker, P.J.H. and van der Heijden, C.A.H.M. (1992) "Integrating Scenarios into Strategic Planning at Royal Dutch/Shell", *Planning Review*, 20(3): 41–6.

Schwartz, P. (1991) *The Art of The Long View: Planning for the future in an uncertain world*. New York: Currency Doubleday.

Schweiger, D.M., Sandberg, W.R. and Ragan, J.W. (1986) "Group Approaches for Improving Strategic Decision Making: A comparative analysis of dialectical inquiry, devil's advocacy, and consensus", *Academy of Management Journal*, 29: 51–71

Schweiger, D.M., Sandberg, W.R. and Rechner, P.A. (1989) "Experiential Effects of Dialectical Inquiry, Devil's Advocacy, and Consensus Approaches to Strategic Decision Making", *Academy of Management Journal*, 32: 745–72.

Taleb, N.N. (2008) *The Black Swan: The Impact of the Highly Improbable*. London: Penguin.

Taleb, N.N. (2009) "Errors, Robustness, and the Fourth Quadrant", *International Journal of Forecasting*, 25: 747–59.

Tetlock, P.E. (2005) *Expert Political Judgment*. Princeton, Princeton University Press.

Tversky, A. and Kahneman, D. (1981) "The Framing of Decisions and the Psychology of Choice", *Science*, 211: 453–8.

Tversky, A. and Kahneman, D. (1983) "Extensional versus Intuitive Reasoning: The conjunction fallacy in probability judgment", *Psychological Review*, 90: 293–315.

UN Global Compact (2007) *The Principles for Responsible Management Education*. New York: United Nations Global Compact Office.

van der Heijden, K. (1996) *Scenarios: The Art of Strategic Conversation*. Chichester: John Wiley.

van der Heijden, K., Bradfield, R., Burt, G., Cairns, G. and Wright, G. (2002) *The Sixth Sense: Accelerating Organizational Learning with Scenarios*. Chichester: John Wiley.

Wack, P. (1985a) "Scenarios: Uncharted waters ahead", *Harvard Business Review*, 63(5): 73–89.

Wack, P. (1985b) "Scenarios: Shooting the rapids", *Harvard Business Review*" 63(6): 139–50.

Walker, W.E., Marchau, V.A.W.J. and Swanson, D. (2010) "Addressing Deep Uncertainty using Adaptive Policies: Introduction to Section 2", *Technological Forecasting & Social Change*, 77: 917–23.

Wardekker, J.A., de Jong, A., Knoop, J.M. and van der Sluijs, J.P. (2010) "Operationalising a Resilience Approach to Adapting an Urban Delta to Uncertain Climate Changes", *Technological Forecasting and Social Change*, 77: 987–98.

Wright, G. and Goodwin, P. (2009) "Decision Making under Low Levels of Predictability: Enhancing the scenario method", *International Journal of Forecasting*, 25: 813–25.

Wright, G., Cairns, G. and Goodwin, P. (2009) "Teaching Scenario Planning: Lessons from practice in academe and business", *European Journal of Operational Research*, 194 (1): 323–35.

Wright, G., van der Heijden, K., Bradfield, R., Burt, G. and Cairns. G. (2004) "The Psychology of Why Organizations can be Slow to Adapt and Change", *Journal of General Management*, 29(4): 21–36.

Wright, G., van der Heijden, K., Burt, G., Bradfield, R. and Cairns, G. (2008) "Scenario Planning Interventions in Organizations: An analysis of the causes of success and failure, *Futures*, 40: 218–36.

Yaniv, I (2011). "Group Diversity and Decision Quality: Amplification and attenuation of the framing effect", *International Journal of Forecasting*, 27: 41–9.

# Index

Printed and bound in Great Britain by
CPI Group (UK) Ltd, Croydon, CR0 4YY